The Secrets Of Magic

Communicational Excellence For The 21st Century

*A Book About The "Magic" Of
Language In Communicating*

by

L. Michael Hall, PhD

Published by Crown House Publishing

First published in the UK by

Crown House Publishing
Crown Buildings
Bancyfelin
Carmarthen
Wales

British Library of Cataloguing-in-Publication Data
A catalogue entry for this book is available
from the British Library.

ISBN 1899836152

Printed and bound in Wales by
WBC Book Manufacturers,
Waterton Industrial Estate,
Bridgend, Mid Glamorgan.

Contents

Charts

Preface

ONCE UPON A TIME an Ugly Frog was Touched by Magic.
A Wizard waved her wand, said some words,
and then, presto ... puff of smoke ...
the ugly frog discovered that he was really ...
A HANDSOME PRINCE
with all the resources he needed
To live fully and vibrantly.
For, you see, the magic of the words restored him
to his true identity and his true destiny
as it opened his eyes to all the rich resources within.
And so he went on his princely way—merrily—
totally Transformed and Thrilled...
And repeatedly Telling his story to all who would listen,
which began to cause him to *feel really curious*
about that magic.
"Just how did she do that anyway?"
"Is there any Method in her Magic?"
"If I could find the Structure in the Magic—
could I then learn to perform Magic like that?"
And these words echoed in his mind.
Now it came to pass in those days
that two modelers were also touched by Magic
And forthwith thereafter began to hold workshops
throughout the Kingdom on the Structure of Magic.
And so as the prince took his place in the workshop,
and not even knowing the extent of his magic skills
having been Touched by Magic,
and so he *accessed his most ferocious learning state*
because he didn't want to miss any of
the secrets of magic.
So as he began to *breath deeply and fully*
with a calm relaxation in the growing excited anticipation
of become even more skilled as
A NEURO-LINGUISTIC MAGICIAN...

Foreword

When you study and work with the Meta-model, you actually work with a model of **profound simplicity**. I didn't know that at first. Actually, after I first learned the Meta-model I really didn't think that much about it. Yes, I liked it. But it didn't ring any bells for me. Having studied several of the biblical languages (koine Greek, Hebrew, along with some Latin) and having studied language itself, including Transformational Grammar and General Semantics, my *first impression* of the Meta-model went, "Yes, I know that stuff; nothing impressive about that."

How amazing that you can hold a magic wand in your hands— *and not know it!*

Then one day I got an attitude adjustment. During my first training with Richard Bandler, I heard Richard say—almost in an off-the-cuff manner—that *everything in NLP*, every model, every technique, and every distinction that makes a difference arises from the Meta-model.

"Oh really?"

He further commented that to *not* know the Meta-model inside out, backwards and forwards, and to understand it as a model of modeling would effectively prevent one from ever becoming truly proficient (let alone a master) with the *technologies of magic* that NLP has given birth to.

Well that caught my attention. From those statements emerged numerous questions within:

"How can he think that this simple model about language could function that powerfully?

What does he know about the Meta-model that I must have overlooked?

What about the Meta-model informs him that it plays that crucial a role in modeling and human experiences?"

At the point that I asked such questions of myself I didn't know the answers. So I returned to the Meta-model and to *The Structure of Magic* to discover the secret of magic that so thrilled Richard Bandler.

Later, after I found the secret, I began exploring for more and additional expressions of such "magic." That led me first back to Korzybski and General Semantics, then to cognitive psychology, linguistics, and a multitude of other places. I eventually even wrote my dissertation on the subject of how language works in seemingly "magical" ways (see *Languaging*, 1996). So as I begin this work, let me suggest that you take care not to miss **the profound nature of the simplicity of the magic** that lies before you in this book. Truly you hold a magic wand in your hands that provides you significant keys to *the secret* of magic.

Writing Caveats

In this *new and improved version of the structure of magic* I have not only written this text *about* languaging for improved science and sanity, I have also sought to *use* and *practice* such languaging in the writing. (If you have a magic wand—you might as well use it.) So, a few caveats to provide warning ahead of time regarding some of **the unique languaging practices** in this book.

You will discover, in the following pages, that I have incorporated numerous linguistic devices from the field of General Semantics. When you first come upon them, they may strike you as strange and weird. Alfred Korzybski (1933/ 1994) developed these as linguistic mechanisms to help promote a more non-Aristotelian language system and orientation. He did that to promote "science and sanity" (hence the name of his classic work). These *extensional devices* include:

1. "Etc."

You will find that I have frequently used "etc." in the following text. This extensional device, from Korzybski and general-semantics, serves to primarily remind us that "we have not said all," and that we "could have said a great deal more." The value of this? To avoid the *absolutism* of assuming that we have uttered the last word about something. So, allow *"etc."* to evoke curiosity and thoughtfulness as you read so that it will cue your brain to start filling in the blanks of all the things that could have been said.

2. *Using verbs in the place of nouns*

Given that we live in *a dynamic universe of processes and actions,* we encode and map this in *verbs* rather than nouns. This makes for a more functional, behavioral, and dynamic language that replaces the old static Aristotelian world-view and language forms. Thus, expect to find "emote" and "emoting" for "emotions," "somatizing" for experiencing psychosomatic results (headaches, stomach aches, ulcers, etc.).

3. *E-Prime*

To eliminate two very unsane forms of linguistic mapping (the "is" of identity and the "is" of predication), I have for the most part *primed* English of the "to be" verbs (is, am, be, being, been, was, were, etc.) that comprise those categories. Sometimes doing this results in some awkward sentences. For more about the E-priming process see Appendix B.

4. *Parenthesis*

I have also put parentheses on terms ("magic," "mind," etc.) to call for special attention to the usage of the word. As another extensional device in General Semantics it highlights terms that we need to treat with extreme care.

5. *Hyphenation*

"Elementalism" begins due to the fact that we can take *an element* of a process or system and pull it apart for conceptual analysis so that we can talk about that facet or part. We do this conceptually and linguistically. But sometimes we forget that the element *only exists in thought and language* and not actually in reality. Such forgetting then leads to *elementalism.* Hence, we talk about "mind" as if it exists apart from "body." We speak about "space" as if it can exist apart from "time." Korzybski recommended sprinkling a little dash here and there in order to reconnect the world, hence "the time-space continuum," "the mind-body organism," "neuro-semantic" reality, etc.

These linguistic devices come from General Semantics and provide a basic **non-Aristotelian language system and orientation**. Korzybski (1933/1994) used this term to refer to a basic epistemological shift from the Aristotelian perceptive of reality in terms of "things" or *substances* to the more modern quantum physics perceptive. Aristotle's 300 BC macroscopic ontology (philosophy of "being") saw the world as comprised of Things, Entities, and Substances. Thus nouns and nominalization dominated language served him well. It also served mankind pretty well until the invention of the microscope. Then with the invention of the electronic microscope and the Einsteinian revolution it really became an ill-formed way of mapping "reality."

The newer non-Aristotelian perspective and language orient us to *a process world* full of energy manifestations rather than things. Korzybski said that the language shift that this implies enables us to talk about **processes** that "never remain the same." This gives us a more functional and behavioral language that induces ongoing changes. In **Figuring Out People: Design Engineering With Meta-Programs**, 1997, I suggested this (along with Bob Bodenhamer) as another meta-program. For a complete study of Non-Aristotelian Systems, see Korzybski's **Science and Sanity**.

Michael Hall
September, 1997

Acknowledgments

I could not have written this book without the initial inspiration from the two geniuses that began the Neuro-Linguistic Model—**John Grinder** and **Richard Bandler**. They charted the way in 1973—1976 as they modeled and made explicit *the Meta-model* in their original ground-breaking volumes, *The Structure of Magic, Volumes I & II.*

Nor could this book have arisen without the scholarship of **Robert Dilts** who has written about and developed the Meta-model as much as anyone, especially in his volumes of *The Roots of NLP* (1983) and *Applications of NLP* (1983).

Further acknowledgment for the theoretical understandings within this work go to **Alfred Korzybski** and his multiple writings in the field of General Semantics, but primary for *Science and Sanity*. Also **George Lakoff**, Noam Chomsky's student and developer of Generative Semantics as well as a pioneer in Cognitive Linguistics.

Bobby G. Bodenhamer and I began working together in 1996 and to date have co-written five books. I have come to depend upon his constant encouragement, insights, excitement, and challenges. If you find the writing straighter, clearer, and more practical— credit goes to him! You will find his hand in the graphics and charts of the Meta-model at the end of chapters 2 and 4 and well as his contribution to our work on the *Mind-Lines Model* in Chapter 6.

Similarly to **Charles Faulkner**, who via e-mail kept me on my toes about "the old model" that this work revisits. Charles, having spent several years studying Generative Semantics and Cognitive Grammar, played a significant role in sharpening my conclusions here—even though they differ very much from his own.

Others who have similarly played a significant role in this work include:

Katrina Patterson who, using her extensive background as an NLP trainer, edited the text to bring it to its current format.

Joe Munshaw and Nelson Zink in their writings in *NLP World* and personal conversations about the Meta-model. While I have "taken to task" many of their ideas, they have certainly offered new perspectives on the Meta-model.

Byron Lewis and **Frank Pucelik** for their creative and insightful work in *Magic Demystified (1982)*.

Joseph O'Connor and John Seymour for their description of the Meta-model in *Introducing Neuro-Linguistic Programming* (1990).

Peter Kean, NLP trainer, also provided me encouragement as well as information about resources within the NLP community. And especially to my publisher, **Dr. Martin Roberts** of the Anglo-American Book Company who has provided constant editorial insight and encouragement throughout. When I get lost in the trees of the details I can always depend upon Martin for the larger perspective that he always provides.

*A special thanks to Science and Behavior Books for granting special permission to extensively quote from **The Structure of Magic, Volume I** (1975) by Richard Bandler and John Grinder, and permitting them to be reprinted here.*

Chapter 1

The Magic Of Symbols

Incantations That Transform Reality

*"They are methods which give an onlooker
the impression of magic
if he be not himself initiated or equally skilled in the mechanism."*
(H. Vaihinger, 1924)

*"Magic is hidden in the language we speak.
The webs that you can tie and untie are at your command
if only you pay attention to what you already have (language)
and the structure of the incantations for growth..."*
(Bandler & Grinder, 1975, p. 19)

In the early 1970s, two modelers stumbled on three magicians. Out of that encounter arose a new field. Today we call that field— **Neuro-Linguistic Programming**, or NLP.

Now the particular magicians that they modeled so happened to have worked their magic in the context of *therapy*. By using words and non-linguistic responses with their clients, somehow, they facilitated a *transformation* in the lives of hurting men and women.

This fascinated the modelers. It evoked many questions in them. They wanted to understand **the structure** of this "magic."

"How do these geniuses communicate in such a way which allows them to have that kind of effect?"

"Does the magic of the metamorphosis lie in the specific words they use, the way they say the words, their supporting non-verbal communications, or what?"

"Can we learn this magic?"

"Can we learn to replicate this magic and train others to do it as well?"

1

The modelers, coming from backgrounds of linguistics, transformational grammar, general-semantics, computer programming, and mathematics approached the field of psychology from an entirely different point of view than that typically held in the field of psychology. Having no investment about the various psychological theories (psychoanalysis, behaviorism, client-centered, humanism, etc.), as they looked at Gestalt, Family Systems, and Hypnotherapy, they assumed that if *they all worked*, (in varying degrees at different times with different clients), then there must exist a meta-level of commonality. This idea then led them to the idea that, **if** they could find *the structure within, behind, and above* the specifics, they could learn the secrets of the magic, and pass them on to others as well. And so they did.

We now call the components of that magic (its structure, process, and the formulas and incantations)—**NLP**. This refers to how we humans become "programmed," so to speak, in our very **neurology** by means of our linguistics (the languages of the "mind").

How does this "programming" occur?

How can we re-program human response patterns?

How does human neuro-linguistics operate?

What principles, laws, and guidelines govern human neuro-linguistics?

How does the communication process itself play into programming?

What processes best allow us to run our brain and neurology and take charge of our programming?

Magic Enters Into A New Millennium

Nearly a quarter of a century has now passed since the 1975 publication of the first work in this field—*The Structure of Magic (Volume I)* by Richard Bandler and John Grinder. Accordingly, it now becomes appropriate to reflect on the NLP movement as a field and the community it generated. With that historical consciousness, we can then ask various questions:

What has happened to **the magic** that the two modelers discovered?

What else has become public knowledge about "the structure of magic" in the ensuing years?

How has the knowledge of that magic grown and developed?

What other pathways and directions has it taken those who have studied this field?

What has happened in the field of linguistics from which the Meta-model arose?

The Original Magic

Richard Bandler and Dr. John Grinder subtitled their original work, *"A Book About Language and Therapy."* Why did they put this emphasis on *therapeutic* language? Because as they discovered the three therapeutic wizards (Fritz Perls, Virginia Satir, and Milton Erickson), and applied their skills of modeling to the language and non-language interventions of these wizards, they happened upon **the very structure of their magic, incantations, and genius**. Once they found that, it didn't take them long to develop their neuro-linguistic model about how human brains and bodies get "programmed" to function, or by application to extend it to fields beyond therapy: education, law, sports, health, medicine, sales, persuasion, etc.

Yet it all started with these wizards, **Fritz Perls, Virginia Satir,** and **Milton Erickson**. First, it started with *Fritz Perls*, the founder of Gestalt Therapy. Richard so happened to have stumbled on Perls while working for Science and Behavior Books in the warehouse. About that time, Fritz Perls died, having just given publisher Dr. Robert S. Spitzer an unfinished manuscript (later published as *The Gestalt Approach and Eye Witness to Therapy*, 1973). Dr. Spitzer asked Richard, though only twenty-one at the time, to finish editing it. The second part consisted of Gestalt Therapy sessions which Richard transcribed from teaching films that Fritz had made,

> *"Again, Richard spent day after day wearing ear phones while watching the films—making certain that the transcription was accurate. He came out of it talking and acting like Fritz Perls. I found myself accidentally calling him Fritz on several occasions."* (Spitzer, 1992, p. 41)

Soon thereafter, even though still a college student, Richard began teaching a class at the University of Southern California on Gestalt Therapy. McClendon (1989) noted in **The Wild Days** that the University granted this privilege to fourth year students.

Richard had a remarkable ability to imitate. When he was asked to audiotape and transcribe a month long workshop by Virginia Satir, Richard quickly developed many of Virginia's voice patterns and mannerisms. Virginia's work introduced him to the psychological and communication field of Family Systems.

Finally, urged on by their neighbor and anthropologist, Gregory Bateson, Richard and John modeled the work of *Milton Erickson*, the founder of Ericksonian hypnotherapy.

Bandler and Grinder experienced these three wizards, as so many others had, as having skills and secrets that seemed "leaps and bounds" ahead of the skills of other therapists. They too experienced their work as

> *"so amazing to watch that it moves us with powerful emotions, disbelief, and utter confusion. Just as with all wizards of the ages of the earth whose knowledge was treasured and passed down from sage to sage—losing and adding pieces but retaining a basic structure—so, too, does the magic of these therapeutic wizards also have structure."* (1975, p. xiii)

The Wild Idea—"Magic Has Structure"

What separated Bandler and Grinder from others who had studied these geniuses of communication and therapy? *They looked for the structure of the magic.* They looked deeper than the surface expressions of sudden release of pain, shift of focus, transformation of emotion, and change of behavior. Beyond the complexity and richness of the processes, they looked for **the ordering syntax of the component pieces** that made the magic work.

Thus they brought to their explorations the scientific attitude of "understanding human behavior by breaking it down into relatively separate areas of study..." (p. 1). In doing this, Bandler and Grinder sought to uncover the structure of human behavior in terms of how it operates in a rule governed way.

Using the discovery of Chomsky (1957), which revolutionized linguistics by replacing Skinner's behaviorism, they utilized the principle of language acquisition and development as *"rule governed"* to explore how words and language can operate in seemingly "magical" ways in human neurology to form "personality," skills, and human mental-and-emotional experiences. For them,

> *"The nervous system which produces digital communication (e. g. language) is the same nervous system which generates the other forms of human behavior ...—analogical communication systems, dreams, etc."* (p. 54)

So they approached these therapeutic wizards with the wild idea that they could learn the structure of their magic, and replicate it. They called this approach **"modeling."** To pull this off, they also brought to this task a very specific attitude—one of passionate (or ferocious) curiosity and interest. About "the magical quality" of Satir and Perls they wrote,

> *"To deny this capacity or to simply label it talent, intuition, or genius is to limit one's own potential as a people-helper."* (p. 6)

Instead they took the attitude that it has structure, like other complex human activities, and that therefore they and others could learn it. They could learn it given the appropriate resources and training.

Using also the seminal map-territory distinction in the work of Alfred Korzybski (1933/ 1994) that we do not operate upon the world directly, but indirectly through our maps (or models) of the world, Bandler and Grinder recognized that **therein lies the magic**. In the very structure and syntax of our words, pictures, sounds, sensations, smells, etc. they found the magic—because *our map(s) powerfully influence and govern all of our experience of the world*. Change the map—and we change our experience of the world. This means that *the map* drives the *magic*. (Now you know one of the meta-secrets about "magic".)

This also describes the place where the therapeutic wizards applied their magic to their clients—not the everyday life experiences of the clients, but their maps. They didn't aim to change the clients' world—only the clients' **model** of the world. And the map-territory interface occurred for the clients via *the communication process*. Thus, as the wizards talked with their clients, they engaged the individuals to describe their plight, answer questions, and think about their understandings, etc. Then, out of that encounter—something happened. Something changed. Suddenly, something felt different. Bandler and Grinder discovered that they could offer a pretty precise description of the change that occurred in the client's representations.

If the *mechanism of transformation* involves **altering one's representational maps** of the world (his or her paradigm), then what *tools* facilitate this change? Bandler and Grinder again pointed to *the communication process*—the set of verbal and non-verbal tools that we all have available. So they modeled Perls, Satir, and Erickson for "a specific set of tools that seem to us implicit in the actions" of these therapists (p. 6). These include the following tools (techniques or technology) from which then arose the Meta-model:

Verbal/Linguistic Change Tools:

- Asking for specificity about a word or phrase:
  When, where, to what extent, with whom, etc.?
  (Unspecified Noun, Verbs, Relational terms, etc.)
- Indexing the referent to time, place, event, person, etc.
  (Deleted references and terms)
- Discovering the process of how something works
  How do you know? (Mind-Reading,
  Complex Equivalence)
  How does X work? (Cause-Effect, Nominalizations)
- Challenging the structure of a word, phrase, or sentence:
  What if you could? (Modal Operator of Impossibility)
  Who says? (Lost Performative)
  What else could it mean? (Complex Equivalence)
  What do you presuppose in that statement?
  (Presuppositions)
- Matching the same kind of words with the speaker
  (pacing).
  (Pacing predicates, value words, etc.)
- Mismatching words to alter representation.
- Using a guided fantasy to journey to new resources.
- Examining congruity/incongruity between para-
  messages (multiple messages on the same logical level)

Non-Verbal Change Tools:

- Pacing the speaker's physiology: breathing, rate of speech,
  posture, gesturing, volume, tone, eye accessing, etc.
- Leading the speaker's physiology.
- Encouraging a re-enactment of the experience.
- Setting up therapeutic double-binds.

The Place Of Magic

If the therapeutic wizards didn't do "real magic," but simply had developed the skills, models, and resources (conscious or unconscious) to create a profound and powerful influence on the hurting minds-and-hearts of clients, then **where** does the "magic" (or impression of magic) actually occur? It occurs in the client's *mapping process itself and in the resultant maps.* More specifically, it occurs in a person's *way of representing* the world.

This accorded with what Vaihinger (1924) wrote half a century earlier. We humans, he said,

> *"hardly notice that we are acting on a double stage—our own inner world ... and also an entirely different and external world."* (p. 160)

He noted that we experience the inner world and then "objectify" it "as the world of sense-perception." Yet it only (and always) exists *as only a map*—a way of *representing* the world.

> *"Each of us creates a representation of the world in which we live—that is, we create a map or model which we use to generate our behavior. Our representation of the world determines to a large degree what our experience of the world will be, how we will perceive the world, what choices we will see available to us as we live in the world."* (p. 7)

Today this paradigm of human functioning locates NLP in the Cognitive-Behavioral Psychology field. It utilizes the constructivist epistemology which the wisdom and genius of Korzybski (1933/ 1994) expressed in his classic map-territory distinction.

> *"A map is not the territory it represents but, if correct, it has a similar structure to the territory, which accounts for its usefulness."* (pp. 58-60)

Here lies **the secret** then to the *magical* powers and interventions of all therapeutic wizards—somehow, in some way, by various techniques, models, parables, myths, etc.—**they effect a change in one's neuro-linguistic maps.** And, given that we *operate* in the world and on the world via our maps—when we change the map, we experience the "magic" of a changed life. This results in changed thinking-feeling, changed behaviors, changed skills, and changed perceptions. The spell of the changed map transforms our internal world into another world. Suddenly, like Dorothy we open the door and realize that "we are no longer in Kansas."

The Nature Of These "Magic" Maps

That human beings operate from an internal "map" of some sort has long been intuited by philosophers (Immanuel Kant, 1787) and psychologists (William James, 1890). Yet only in the twentieth century have researchers and theorists honed in more and more specifically on the nature of these internal maps.

Korzybski (1933/ 1994) developed his epistemological model about the working and processing of human neurological abstracting. He published it in *Science and Sanity* in numerous forms—most notably *the structural differential,* a diagram illustrating the logical levels of abstraction that differentiate our abstracting maps from the territory. This model analyzes how the human nervous system interacts with the world at various levels and follows the abstracting process from the territory in its energy manifestations on the sense receptors to the internal "maps" that resulted at different levels.

Piaget (1926, 1936/1952) referred to innate *schemas* (or structures) of the "mind" in his study of the development of cognitive skills over the life-span, structures by which we represent, reason with, integrate, and attach meaning to events.

Bartlett (1932) introduced the term *schema* into Behavioral Psychology to indicate some kind of internal *intervening* mechanism (or map) between stimulus and response to explain human learning and responding.

Kelly (1955) describe our maps as "personal constructs" that guide, govern, and determine internal experiencing, construction of meaning, emoting, etc.

By the time of the Cognitive Revolution in psychology, dated from the work of George Miller, Ulrich Neisser, Bruner, et al. in 1956, the idea that internal maps governed human experience had become well accepted. About the same time Chomsky (1957) delivered the death-blow to Skinner's Behaviorism in his analysis of language acquisition when he demonstrated the total inadequacy of the association theories as an explanatory model about "verbal behavior."

Yet what actually comprises these internal *maps, schemas, constructs, etc.?* Or, to ask the question that Bateson (1972) raised, *"What actually gets mapped onto the map?"* Obviously, these terms (map, schema, paradigm) do not *literally* describe anything in the brain. They only metaphorically describe the neurological processing of "information" in terms of representation. Yet even "representation" gets us no closer to anything literal. We only "phenomenologically" have a sense of "representation." Bateson finally concluded,

> *"What gets onto the map, in fact, is difference, ... and what is a difference? ... It is certainly not a thing, or an event ... A difference is an abstract matter. ... The territory never gets in at all. The territory is Ding an sich [Thing in itself] and you can't do anything with it. Always the process of representation will filter it out so that the mental world is only maps of maps of maps, ad infinitum. All 'phenomena' are literally 'appearances.' ...what gets from territory to map is transforms of difference and these differences are elementary ideas."* (1972, pp. 451-457)

Bandler and Grinder chose to simply go with the phenomenological idea of *representation* as "good enough" for the purposes they had in mind. So even though we do not *literally* have pictures, sounds, sensations, etc. in our cortex, and even though we have no *literal* "screen" in our head wherein we *re-present* to ourselves what we have seen, heard, and felt via our sense receptors—this *phenomenological "sense"* of such seems to work well enough to explain the magic *at that level*. If we change our representations at the level of our sensed representations, our nervous system uses its out-of-conscious neurological processes to respond differently.

So starting there, Bandler and Grinder presented the "experience and perception as an active process" and analyzed the neurological, social, and individual constraints that play a significant role in our map-making (1975, pp. 8-20). In this analysis, they quoted scientific experiments that led them to conclude that,

> *"our whole nervous system systematically distorts and deletes whole portions of the real world. This has the affect of reducing the range of possible human experiences as well as introducing differences between what is actually going on in the world and our experience of it. Our nervous system, then, initially determined genetically, constitutes the first set of filters which distinguish the world—the territory—from our representations of the world—the map." (p. 9)*

Quoting Huxley (1954) about "the reducing valve of the brain and nervous system" Bandler and Grinder highlighted **several constraints on our map-making**. These include the *neurological* constraints in our sense receptors and neurological structure, the *social* constraints that arise from living in communities, and the *individual* constraints that uniquely distinguish us.

Under *the social constraints* that affect our map-making, they relied upon sociological and anthropological studies. Language itself, as well as all of the social filters of beliefs and ideas, powerfully affect what we can perceive and how we generate internal representations. The social constraints involve the cultural presuppositions coded in the language, the beliefs and values of the society, etc.

Korzybski noted the affect of a culture's language on the nervous system (especially all Aristotelian cultures) in *"the is of predication."* If we say, "The book is blue" we use a linguistic category ("blue") that constrains our thinking and perceiving and may even become confused in thinking that the *name* that we give to the sensation *"is"* the same as the sensation. Yet "blueness" occurs as a socially conditioned response given the English language system, our attribute—not the territory.

> *"All that is given to consciousness is sensation. By adding a Thing to which sensations are supposed to adhere as attributes, thought commits a very serious error. It hypostatizes sensation, which in the last analysis is only a process, as a subsistent attribute, and ascribes this attribute to a thing that either exists only in the complex of sensations itself, or has been simply added by thought to what has been sensed.... Where is the sweet that is ascribed to the sugar? It exists only in the act of sensation..."*
> (Vaihinger, 1924, p. 167)

No wonder we end up with models of the world that can differ so much from the world! And yet the difference does not end there. We also have to consider **the individual constraints** that influence each of us as we generate our own unique maps. We all experience a unique personal history—"no two life histories will ever be identical." (p. 12).

Each of these three constraints on human mapping works in a systemic way. This means that the *products* of each domain re-enter the process to effect the functioning of the other domains. The beliefs and values that we develop individually and socially become perceptual filters at the neurological level. They create our habits of thought, emotion, speech, perceiving, and relating. They reinforce the cultural maps that we have received, thus confirming our "reality."

What then shall we say about the *nature* of our maps? We all have, and use, as we operate in the world, a map *of* reality that radically differs from the territory. None of us deal with reality as such— only "reality" filtered and coded through ideas and beliefs. In these maps, we have **deleted** information to avoid feeling overwhelmed. We have created **generalizations** to summarize and synthesize patterns in order to cope. We have **distorted** other data according to our neurological, cultural, and individual constraints. By the very *nature of our maps*, then, we inevitably operate from schemas, paradigms, and frames of references that *differ* from the territory. Some of these enhance our life experiences, some of these severely limit us.

We can rephrase Korzybski's "the map is not the territory" using a different content, *"The menu is not the meal."* Recognizing a menu as "a menu," and distinct from the meal that it references, plays a very important role if we want to make a good adjustment to the reality of eating, wouldn't you say? Generally, we don't consider people very "sane" who go to the restaurant and consume the menu. Nor will their nervous system tolerate that kind of a mistake for long!

Transforming The Magic

Where do "problems," distresses, and conflicts arise? Human *"problems"* actually arise primarily from **the discord** between our internal maps and the territory they reference. The map we use to guide simply does not serve us well in that we can't go where we desire or experience what we want to experience. This discord may reflect **several kinds of mapping problems**.

1. *Inaccurate maps.* The discord may arise because we have a menu that very inaccurately represents the territory—when the waiter brings us what we think we ordered, the difference between the two shocks our system and "throws us for a loop" (to use an Americanism). No one has, or can have, a perfectly accurate map. We *have to* delete, generalize, and distort to create a map. So all maps suffer varying degrees of inaccuracy. Nor does inaccuracy, in and of itself, make a map worthless or unreliable. Some inaccuracies can serve us very well. Mapping problems arise from having a false-to-fact map in a critical area which, in turn, *disorients* us. Therefore it fails to provide us a good guide.

2. *Inadequate maps.* As with inaccuracy, all of our maps suffer varying degrees of inadequacies. In navigating geography, we have many different kinds of geographical maps, each one offering different levels of adequacy for different kinds of purposes and functions. Thus while we would find a topographical map adequate for mountain climbing, it probably would not prove adequate for driving around town.

We probably work from an inadequate map when we pick up the short version of a menu and only see three choices, when actually the full menu includes hundreds of items. While we could have had much more, our menu provided us no such hint.

3. **Distorted maps.** Sometimes a map simply gets it all wrong. They not only leave out streets and roads that could have made our trip shorter, but they link one road to another that doesn't exist. So off we go on pseudo-treasure hunts! Someone penned in "Fountain of Youth," as a joke on the map and then forgot to erase it. A major map distortion shows up in the Aristotelian maps, "What you see and perceive is not a map, but real." Bandler and Grinder wrote,

> *"What we have found is not that the world is too limited or that there are no choices, but that these people [who come for therapy] block themselves from seeing those options and possibilities that are open to them since they are not available in their models of the world."* (p. 13)

What primarily governs our experiences in life? What determines how we perceive, think, feel, act, and relate? **The *quality and richness* in our representations of the world.** So, generally speaking, the richer our map, the more accurate, adequate, and useful our menu—the more choices we have. The more impoverished our model—the fewer our choices.

The central psychological issue then in "human nature" does not fall back to the idea that people simply "are" bad, crazy, demonic, or sick. No. The central psycho-logical issue involves *the quality and richness of the maps* people use in navigating life. Generally, people make the best choices they have. They do so from the options available to them in their model of the world. If the only set of choices on the menu consists of baked, fried, or raw worms—people choose from that frame-work.

Just because someone yells when upset, feels defensive when criticized, feels guilty about feeling afraid, etc. does not make them "crazy." They may simply lack a richly focused model of the world that empowers them with much more resourceful responses.

14

"... human beings' behavior, no matter how bizarre it may first appear to be, makes sense when it is seen in the context of the choices generated by their model." (p. 14)

What drives (or controls) the quality and richness of our maps?— Our ability to manipulate symbols, that is, to create models. If we *over-generalize* in our map-making—we create limitations (eliminate alternative choices) for how we can act upon the world. We typically over-generalize by making "rules" for living and fail to contextualize them: "Don't touch hot stoves." "Rocky chairs are unstable." "Don't express feelings." We over-generalize by seeing things in all-or-nothing terms. "No one ever gives me a break."

We create limiting maps (in quality and richness) by *deleting* information and dimensions of the world. We filter out representations, ideas, concepts, understandings, etc. that could enrich us and that could make a difference in perceiving and acting. So we move through the world *without the empowering strategies* that allow us to resolve conflicts respectfully, explore new options, invent new ideas, get over the past, etc. We discount things by bringing in various criteria so that we don't even notice.

We also manipulate symbols by *distorting*. This can enrich our lives (as in fantasy and creative imagination), yet it can also limit when we distort the world via beliefs about causation and meaning. "He *makes* me feel afraid by yelling at me." "When she doesn't look at me when I talk, I know she thinks I'm stupid." "I'll never get over that hurt!" "You just can't teach old dogs new tricks."

When we add these map-making processes together so that we generalize a rule which thereby deletes information to the contrary, we end up with a map that forbids and prevents us from **updating our map.** Now that does generally have some value— we can stop inputting new information, erasing parts of the map that we discovered incorrect, and staying tentative to new corrective information. Yet we pay for this "peace," "sense of security," and "comfort" by moving through the world with a closed and rigid map that becomes more and more out-dated and irrelevant every day. Not exactly the best kind of guide to have in moving through an ever-changing environment. A rigid map like that will typically *not* serve us very well. It will only make us closed to new information. It will limit our choices, and generate dis-empowering perspectives.

If human "problems" then lie in our maps—so do human "solutions." By *re-mapping* we can develop a better guide for governing how we think, feel, and act. If our cognitive-emotive schemas wrongly orient us in the world of things, people, and tasks—then hope comes by *restructuring our cognitions* (e. g. our beliefs, values, understandings, paradigms, etc.). Adopting a new schema offers us new ways of orienting ourselves in the world. Bandler and Grinder said this describes what the therapeutic wizards that they modeled did,

> *"They introduce changes in their clients' models which allow their clients more options in their behavior. What we see is that each of these wizards has a map or model for changing their clients' models of the world—i. e., a Meta-model—which allows them to effectively expand and enrich their clients' models in some way that makes the clients' lives richer and more worth living."*
> (p. 18)

Over the years of working with hurting people who seemed to lack the rich quality needed in their maps to live fully, the thera-peutic wizards (Perls, Satir, and Erickson) developed a model about the linguistic models that their clients expressed. This Meta-model empowered them to know *what to go for*—what distinctions they didn't make, what data they had deleted, where the maps created limitations for them, etc.

Transformational Grammar

Dr. John Grinder not only had extensive experience with the Chomskian model of transformational grammar, but had already contributed to that field. Thereafter both he and Richard relied heavily upon that model for their terminology, insights, and model. Even the casual reader can see this in the extensive Appendix A in *The Structure of Magic*, "A Brief Outline of Transformational Grammar."

Yet other than terminology for the Meta-model distinctions (hence the loading up of NLP with linguistic jargon: TDS, complex equivalence, nominalizations, modals, etc.), transformational grammar primarily contributed to the Meta-model by offering a logical level system. It offered a distinction between two levels: Surface Structure (SS) statements and Deep Structure (DS). Almost every writer, researcher, and developer of the NLP model utilized and relied upon this two-fold distinction. Lewis and Pucelik's (1982) work, *Magic Demystified*, exemplifies the amount of dependence on transformational grammar that we find in subsequent presentations of the Meta-model. They devoted a two paragraph box to "Transformational Grammar" (p. 73). And their primary focus—the logical level distinctions coded as SS and DS.

> *"A contemporary school of linguistics proposes a relationship between what is spoken or written by an individual and some deeper internal linguistic representation. The production of a sentence, the actual sound or written sequence of symbols and phrases, is called the surface structure (SS). The deep structure (DS) is also a system of symbols and phrases, but it is much more complex and abstract. The DS is the complete linguistic representation of a person's experience which might be considered the intent or thought behind the SS sentence."*

Accordingly, while originally derived from *Transformational Grammar*, the Meta-model quickly moved on from there. As it did, it *only retained the logical level structure* that we also find in General Semantics regarding various levels of abstraction. Since that time Chomsky has radically changed many facets of his original model. George Lakoff along with other disciples of Chomsky created Generative Semantics, then that field lost steam as "The Linguistic Wars" (Harris, 1993) occurred. Today Cognitive Grammar and Cognitive Linguistics have replaced much of the original Transformational Grammar model. What does this mean for the Meta-model? Rather than write such a volume, I have briefly noted some of these developments in Appendix A. There I have explained how the Meta-model does **not** depend upon transformational grammar for its validity or usefulness.

As a student of Chomsky, Ray Jackendoff has in the past two decades become one of the few scholars to continue the transformational grammar tradition. In his book, **Patterns in the Mind: Language and Human Nature** (1994), he presented the following definition that simplifies it along with some qualifications about misunderstandings about "Deep Structure."

> *"This is one of the foundational ideas behind Chomsky's theory of transformational grammar: a sentence in the mind has an 'underlying structure' or 'deep structure' that is different from its surface form, and various principles of mental grammar can transform the sentence by moving certain parts such as wh-words around."* (p. 77)

> *"Deep structure (now often termed 'D-structure') has always been understood simply as an aspect of syntactic structure that expresses certain structural regularities. These regularities, since they include word order, have to be syntactic (i. e. distinct from meaning) and have to express variation among languages (i. e. they are not universal). However, because of the way deep structure was characterized at a certain stage of development of the theory during the mid and late 1960s, many commentators erroneously identified it with either meaning or Universal Grammar or both. However, this was never the intent of the term, except in certain circles for a certain brief time."* (p. 77)

Conclusion

Neuro-semantic "magic" lies hidden in our words, language, and symbol systems. This "magic" bridges the gulf between the external world and our experience on the inside of the world. Since we do not deal with the world directly, but only through neurological and linguistic transforms of the world—*everything depends upon our maps.* Wave a magic wand over the maps so that we change our abstractions (generalizations) of the world, then we delete different things, notice different things, create different distortions—and presto, we enter into a new and different world.

The maps we use to navigate the world operate only as a guidance mechanism. We don't need to evaluate these mechanisms as "right" or "wrong" so much as evaluate whether they enhance or limit us in our journeys. The NLP Meta-model that follows in the next chapter essentially provides **a map for thinking about our cognitive maps**. It provides a way to listen for, and detect, human maps. It offers ways to challenge them in ways that can elicit richer and more useful maps. The design? To increase human resourcefulness by increasing our awareness of our choices.

Chapter 2

Meta-Model Magic

Understanding The Structure Of Magic

"There's method in the magic."
(L. Michael Hall)

"Magic" occurs *in the symbolic language systems* that we use. By the various language systems (linguistics, math, music, the sensory representational systems, etc.) we *construct* our realities. We weave the webs that comprise our subjective experiences. So the more clarity we have about our understandings about such maps (i. e. how we build them, how they work, what drives them, how to alter them, etc.) the more we can empower ourselves to work with that "magic" (i. e. neuro-linguistic magic), to cast spells, to break old incantations that imprison, and to invent new spells for magic.

If "magic" arises from the way that we conceptually picture the world—then clarity about

> *how* we create our conceptual pictures, the map-making processes that we use,
> how this shows up in language (linguistic markers of poor-mapping)
> and how via language we can re-map to enrich them

endows us with a new option. It empowers us to **design engineer** our lives. Further, this now allows us to consciously choose and design the kind of cognitive maps that will enhance our lives.

In other words, "understanding" (a cognitive map itself) how our maps work, how they arise, how we can alter them (even totally transform them), and how such alteration then effects changes in our perceiving, emoting, talking, behaving, skills, etc. **empowers us to become *magicians* over our own neuro-semantic reality.** (You might want to highlight that last line—it represents a major *secret* of magic.)

Our *map* of mapping (a meta-map) as we have described first raises our appreciation of the importance and value of a meta-map or Meta-model. As such, a Meta-model offers us a higher level understanding about the whole mapping-process and how to effectively manage it. You can think about the Meta-model as itself *a magic wand* by which we can catch, break, and cast spells.

This underscores the realization that "the magic" has structure. To the uninitiated it may seem that the moves (the "sleight of mouth" maneuvers, see *Glossary*) of the therapeutic magicians happens "out of the blue" and without rhyme or reason. But no. *Method does exist in the magic.* And this method the Meta-model of language makes explicit.

Neuro-Semantic Reality—Neuro-Semantic Magic

Using the Meta-model empowers us to become *magicians* over *neuro-semantic reality*. What in the world does this phrase mean? Let's analyze it before proceeding.

Semantic signifies *"meaning."* In Chapter 1 I noted that *meaning* lies *inside* us, and not inside words or symbols. The *meaning* of anything depends upon what ideas we associate with what other ideas or things. In human *subjective* experiences (the only kind of experiences that can exist), when one thing gets connected or associated with another—it does so *inside* our nervous system via our neurology. Hence, Korzybski invented the hyphenated phrase, **neuro-semantics**.

"What does any particular thing mean to you?" "What does 'insult' mean?" It all depends upon what sights, sounds, sensations, etc. you have associated with that term? "What does 'joy' mean?" Again, what have you connected, neurologically, to that word? "What qualifies as a pleasure to you?"

Meaning does not occur apart from, or independent of, human beings. We can't see, hear, feel, smell, or taste "meaning" in the world. It does not exist there. It exists only and solely in the functioning of a given human nervous system. Or, if we want to talk about "shared meanings," then it exists as the shared significances and associations that lots of humans experience with regard to the same referent or object.

Our neuro-semantics consist of the mapping that we have coded and programmed into our body and nervous system. It makes itself known as we *react* (kinesthetically, emotionally, and mentally) to various triggers or stimuli. *Semantic Reactions* (Korzybski's terminology) refer to such reactions that occur automatically, unconsciously, and habitually. *Semantic Responses,* by way of contrast, refer to those responses that we make consciously, thoughtfully, and by choice—a much more human way to live.

Going Meta To Our Model Of The World

Given the gap between the territory of the world and our maps of that territory, it becomes evident that we *always* and *only* relate to the world via some cognitive model. Where we go, how we go, and the quality of the journey that we make in the world depends entirely upon the quality of our maps. Yet every map that we create inevitably leaves things out (deletion), sums up a lot of details into more global configurations (generalization), and radically changes things (distortion). These map-making processes inevitably affect the resulting maps.

To imagine, pretend, or believe that we operate upon the world apart from the abstracting of our nervous system that creates maps describes a very simplistic map that confuses map and territory. Korzybski described that style of reasoning as *Aristotelian thinking/reasoning*. At the heart of that kind of primitive and undifferentiating thinking lies *identification*. This refers to how we can *identify* the territory with some term, name, or word that we use as we reference the territory and then forget that our symbol does not exist *as* the referent itself, but only as a symbol of it. Infants, children, primitive peoples, and animals do however so use their nervous systems. They confuse map and territory. They *identify*. For them, the word "is" the referent. The menu "is" the meal.

When we move beyond the Aristotelian level to Non-Aristotelian thinking, we recognize (and even feel) the difference between map and territory. We recognize that "whatever we say a thing is, *it is not*." Our language maps do not exist as the territory. Stating it in this fashion makes it obvious. *Identity* does not exist. Rather, in the world of processes, only *difference* exists, and difference at every moment. Bateson described difference as "the basic component of mind." Once we deeply incorporate this awareness into our neurology, it gives us a sense of distance from our maps. And that, in turn, enables us to recognize them *as maps.*

Going meta to our models of the world allows us to evaluate them in terms of their value and usefulness. It allows us to recognize them as a rule-governed or structural system. The grammar of any given language system simply comprises the set of rules that describes the well-formed patterns in that language. Going meta allows us to *reflect* on our languages as maps—to detect, identify, and realize how we have linguistically left out characteristics as we have abstracted, generalized specific instances to create classes and classifications of experiences, and distorted or altered things.

Languaging—
A Representation System For "Thinking" And Modeling

The basic *modes* (modalities) by which we "think" involve how we use our internal *representations* of sights, sounds, sensations, smells, tastes, etc. (designated in NLP as "VAK" as a shorthand for the three predominant senses—Visual, Auditory, and Kinesthetic). These basic modalities of awareness comprise our primary thinking. Then as a meta-representation system—we use words.

Using words enables us *to comment on* the things we see, hear, and feel. First we use **sensory-based or descriptive words**. These let us speak with clarity, precision, and specificity about the see, hear, feel referents. As symbols, they allow us to "point to" and reference empirical realities (at the macro-level at least). Yet, inasmuch as the abstraction process does not cease there, we next move to yet another higher level to model those descriptive, empirical words with more abstract ones. This creates and introduces into language **evaluative words**.

Recognizing that we both "think" and model (create mental maps) via our neurological modalities (VAK), sensory-based language, and evaluative based language—we can now employ these **components** of subjectivity to create *an effective technology* that can empower us in hearing language patterns whereby we can recognize the structure of human maps.

How do we do this? By simply paying attention to our internal representations as we hear (or use) language. Having done that, we can then *directly track over from* words to pictures, sounds, movements, etc. on the "screen of our mind." I like to designate this as **representational testing** (or tracking) inasmuch as we essentially use our sensory-based representations to track and then test things. Bandler and Grinder (1975) offered this experience,

> "Read the following sentence, then close your eyes and form a visual image of what the sentence represents. 'I'm afraid!' Now examine your image. It will include some visual representation of the client and some representation of the client's being afraid. Any detail beyond these two images was supplied by you." (p. 58)

How do you make "sense" out of the words, "I'm really depressed!" What internal representations do you use? By noticing how you represent words, ideas, stories, etc., you can begin to become conscious of the internal pictures, words, sounds, and sensations by which you "make sense" of language. This brings your unconscious processing of language into conscious awareness.

This also typically takes some practice. Most people seem to focus consciousness so much on **the content** of their thoughts that they have almost no awareness of its **structure**. (No wonder they can't do neuro-linguistic magic! They don't even *hear* the spells cast on them!) Our "minds" bypass *the form* of the message as it rushes to its *content* which we exclusively equate to its "meaning." So we hear a nominalization like "depression" (a verb turned into a noun) and quickly "make sense" of the language by using our own meanings *without even noticing* the sensory-based representations we use in processing it or the lack of sensory-based information in the word. Yet *if* we do not think about our form of representation, we will likewise not think about the speaker's representations. We will assume correspondence. This, of course, leads to pseudo-understanding, miscommunication, and projection. It leads to hallucinating meaning, blindly receiving hypnotic communications, and easily getting duped.

By careful listening to only the words given and then using *only* those words to *construct a representation* of it, we begin the Meta-modeling process. By basing our representations *only* on the words given, we can **test** for missing information. Actually meta-modeling operates by using *a "Know Nothing" frame of reference*. This enables us to curiously explore until we obtain the high quality information needed. We can explore like the TV detective, Columbo, in asking questions that challenge surface expressions until we get to the deep structures.

As we **representationally test language**, we develop consciousness of how we "represent" words. This enables us to explore our own consciousness in terms of where our brain goes in response to words and what references it uses. We can then use this process for asking high quality information gathering questions about *their meanings*.

One "tool" will especially *not* work with a person who has deleted key information from his or her model of the world. Namely, **advice**! Giving advice to *tell* someone what to do typically "falls into the gaps created by deletion in the client's model." In other words, the advice typically will not even make sense because the person's map of the world doesn't include the structures to receive it. We should therefore keep our advice to ourselves until the person's model becomes rich enough to encompass it. This also highlights the importance of facilitating another's *active involvement* in examining, challenging, and expanding his or her own model of the world. So we use questions—*questions* that invite the person to "go inside" to his or her fuller map comprised of referent experiences (both conscious and unconscious) in order to reconnect to that experience. In doing so, the person can re-map in more accurate, appropriate, and enhancing ways.

Two Kinds Of "Magic"

Having mentioned that we have two basic categories for sorting linguistic patterns, this alerts us to two different kinds of "magical" things that we can do with such categories. **Sensory-based language** primarily describes "things"—objects in the external world. **Evaluative-based language,** by way of contrast, primarily describes *the attributions of values and meanings* that we give to things, processes, and ideas. Accordingly, such language takes us into the realm of non-things (i. e. concepts, abstractions, relationships, and processes). Because these referents concern *mental* constructs, they deal with things inside the nervous system (i. e. understandings, beliefs, evaluations, etc.).

Representationally testing and tracking language enables us to distinguish between these different levels of language. For example, the phrase, "You look angry..." uses *non-sensory* language. It does not describe anything about a person's looks. We cannot videotape that. The statement expresses a speaker's *evaluations*, understandings, and perceptions about some unspecified looks. What does "anger" look, sound, or feel like in behavioral, facial, muscular, or action terms? Notice the difference in the phrase,

> "I notice that you have not made eye contact with me and talk in a lower than usual..."

This sensory based language provides an immediate referent by *describing*, in contrast with *evaluative* language. This statement gives no interpretation of what those action words mean to the speaker. Clarifying the linguistics and meanings (semantics) that we hear empowers us to language with more clarity, precision, and accuracy. It also helps when sharing meanings (evaluations, interpretations) because conceptual language inevitably makes evaluations. By contrast, sensory-based language merely describes.

A simple way to express ourselves without coming across with "judgments" involves shifting to *descriptive language.* Descriptive language pushes fewer "buttons." So most people experience it as less offensive. This describes the "magic" of descriptive languaging for communicating with less abrasion.

> "I could hear you better if you didn't wave your index finger in my face."

Evaluative language typically pushes buttons because it judges and evaluates. This makes that kind of language more provocative.

> "I can't hear you because you talk down to me and insult me with your superiority attitude."

When we language with evaluative statements people typically feel that it "imposes" meanings on them or invites them to try on new meanings which may enhance their lives. In the first case, people will typically respond with resistance, denial, opposition, rejection, etc. In the second, they will access a hypnotic state of suggestibility. We can perform all kinds of magic—both "black magic" and "white magic"—by using evaluative language patterns.

Hypnotic "magic" occurs with evaluative languaging. Non-sensory based language, lacking immediate referents, inherently invites people to go inside to make up their own referents. By not providing sensory-based referents, people develop an internal focus in order to to mentally construct the referents as they seek to make sense of our words. This invites them to "hallucinate" about our communications which therefore induces trance states. If you hear someone say, "Sally became depressed when Bob rejected her", the unspecified verbs provide no detailed picture, sound, or feeling for "rejected." This invites us to supply them. Whatever referents we access to make sense of "rejection" involves *our meanings* and projections. Bob could have raised his voice with her, slapped her face, dated someone else, cussed her out, etc. Whatever references we thought of—we *generated from out of our model of the world.* This identifies how the very nature of language hypnotizes. In fact, all language hypnotizes in that it uses symbols that invite us to "go inside," access our own memory banks (reference structures), and use them to make sense. This puts us in an altered state.

As we can distinguish language using these two categories, we understand why we find "naming" actual existing *things* useful, whereas when we *name* "ideas" and "concepts" this typically creates *fuzziness*. Sensory-based names and terms appropriately name items to which we can refer and even point to. This allows us to agree on the referent. But "naming" a way of conceptualizing something or a process of interactions (a set of relatings) usually does not give a specific referent. It doesn't give clearly defined referents. This creates more opportunities for miscommunication.

For example, does the phrase, "the law of gravity," describe or evaluate? What do we have in this phrase? We have an abstraction or idea. We have a linguistic conclusion that someone has made from some observations.

We certainly can see an apple fall from a tree. We may also hear it, feel it, etc., but we cannot see, hear, feel, smell or taste "the law of gravity." Before Newton saw the apple fall—so had many hundreds and thousands and millions of other people. But Newton drew a conclusion mentally. He created a generalization about a relationship between objects and their movement downward to the surface of the planet. His **idea** related to the apple's falling and described **the relationship** between the apple and the ground. It describes *the process* of the apple moving from one place to another. But the "law" of gravity and "gravity" does not exist as "things" outside our nervous systems; only "falling objects" exist there. This abstraction indicates a conception that we generate within **about** such external objects and events.

The Meta-model that follows enables us to more and more clearly make these distinctions between the territory, and the various levels of mapping (abstracting) that we make about that world.

The Meta-Model Of Language

When Bandler and Grinder molded their model from transformational linguistics, they applied it, first of all, to the context of therapy. As they did this, they chose to highlight the three modeling processes (deletion, generalization, and distortion) and to designate the linguistic structures that fit those formats.

They recognized that the processes people go through in communicating experiences involve the same modeling processes used to create models in the first place. Therefore if we listen to the linguistic forms in the everyday expressions, this gives us the ability (at a meta-level) to recognize problematic mapping distinctions.

> *"The processes by which people impoverish their representation of the world are the same processes by which they impoverish their expression of their representation of the world. The way that people have created pain for themselves involves these processes. Through them they have created an impoverished model. Our Meta-model offers a specific way to challenge these same processes to enrich their model."* (p. 46)

Linguistic Deletions

1. *Simple Deletions*: characteristics left out (Del.)

2. *Comparative and Superlative Deletions:* unspecified relations (CD/SD)

3. *Unspecified Referential Indices*: unspecified Nouns and Verbs (UN/ UV)

4. *Unspecified Processes*—Adverbs Modifying Verbs (UP-adv.)

5. *Unspecified Processes*—Adjectives Modifying Nouns (UP-adj.)

In deleting information, we leave things out as we selectively pay attention to certain dimensions of experience. As we do, we exclude or filter out others elements. We delete in order to prevent ourselves from feeling overloaded with stimuli. Yet we often delete important data. So we need to ask ourselves, "Does this deleting help or hinder me?" Deletion reduces the world to proportions we feel capable of handling. By it we create a reduced and more manageable version of reality.

All deletions do not create problems. We have well-formed deletions when we have *sufficient redundancy* in the immediate context to account for the deletion. Without such redundancy, a model results that lacks the needed specificity for navigating the territory efficiently. A professional communicator needs the ability to hear deletions as they occur and to recover the valuable deleted information.

Under *deletion*, we look for expressions in language indicating missing pieces that create an impoverished cognitive model that thereby leads to limited behavioral options. The following meta-questions help:

> Does this expression offer a complete enough representation?
> Does anything seem missing in this expression?
> What could I guess would fill in the missing pieces?
> If I made a mental videotape from just these words—would I have a clear and detailed movie or would I find vague and unfocused areas?

1. Simple Deletions

Take, as an example, the statement, "People scare me." Here the word "people" does not pick out anyone in particular for reference. The surface expression has simply left out (deleted) the referential index. The over-generalized class term, "people," leaves the listener with too broad a map. We need to index it more specifically. *"Who specifically scares you?"* Our design in asking this? To *bring clarity* to the person's model of the world. Accordingly, as the person re-connects his generalizations with the original experience(s), he or she will produce a fuller expression. "My father scares me."

> "I was told not to do that."—*Told by whom?*
> "I'm confused." *About what?*
> "She's so happy." *Who specifically feels happy?*
> > "The people," "the government," "the Geography class," "capitalists," "liberals," etc.

2. Unspecified Referential Indices (Unspecified Nouns and Verbs)

When the person says, "My father scares me," while we now have the referents (the speaker and his father), the unspecified verb ("scares") provides no clear image of *how the experience takes place*. So we next inquire, "How does your father scare you?" This challenges the unspecified verb with the aim of recovering the deleted information.

The surface expressions of the person offers *a reduced version* of the person's full experience in the world. Frequently this impoverished model limits the person's life in a way that creates "pain." With regard to verbs, every verb suffers from some deletion and so has different degrees of specificity. We should therefore examine them for how much clarity of image they convey.

> *"Ask yourself whether the image presented by the verb in its sentence is clear enough for you to visualize the actual sequence of events being described."* (p. 91)

With unspecified verbs, we can simply ask for a more completely specified verb. *"How specifically did X occur?"*

These include nouns and pronouns, statements that have no immediate referent, or an unclear referent. The speaker has deleted an object, person, event in making a statement. Here we challenge the unfocused statement by reconnecting the words with the referent. "That's not important." *Important to whom? In what way?* "They always get in my way." *Who/what specifically get in your way?*

Unspecific verbs lack a referential index so they do not completely specify their objects. In language, because verbs describe processes, they represent the most dynamic part. Yet when people make the verbal process vague and unspecific, this leaves the listeners guessing how the process occurs. This invites people to hallucinate—to make up their own meanings.

To test unspecified verbs, make an image of the information given and ask yourself whether you can clearly visualize the actual sequence of described events.

"He really frustrates me." *How specifically?*

"She hurt me deeply?" *How did she hurt you specifically? In what way?*

3. Comparative and Superlative Deletions (Unspecified Relations)

In the statement, "He's a lot scarier." We have a comparison suggested, but not specified. *"Scarier than whom?"* (Comparatives and superlatives typically show up in adjectives that end in *er* (faster, better), *est* (fastest, best), or *more/less* (more interesting, less important). The challenge: *"Compared to what?" "With respect to what?"*

To speak in over-generalized terms that deletes important distinctions creates what Korzybski termed "an intensional orientation in the world." To index the specific referents thereby clarifies the model and creates "an extensional orientation." Bandler and Grinder noted this and built this into the Meta-model.

"An extensional definition of a set is one which specifies what the members of the set are by simply listing (i. e. enumerating) them; an intentional definition of a set is one which specifies what the members of the set are by giving a rule or procedure which sorts the world into members and non-members of the set. For example, the set of all humans over six feet in height who live in Ozona, Texas, can be given extentially [actually, extensionally] by a list of the people, who, in fact, live in Ozona, Texas, and are taller than six feet, or intentionally [actually, intensionally] by a procedure, for example:

> *(a) Go to the official directory of residents of Ozona, Texas.*
> *(b) Find each person on the list and determine whether he is taller than two yardsticks placed end to end.*

Korzybski (1933, Chapter 2) has an interesting discussion of this distinction. Notice that, in general, lists or a set specified extentionally [extensionally] have referential indices while sets intentionally [intensionally] given have no referential index." (p. 56)

Structurally, after nouns and verbs come *relational-words* that provide relational descriptions, propositions, and functions. These words do not map out "things" but *concepts* (abstractions) regarding how the subjects/objects relate to other subjects/objects. Such words as "better, best, faster, good, evil, superior, before, after, during," etc. code these relationships.

Accordingly, when someone offers you a relational term that lacks specificity so that you cannot representationally track the term and generate a clear, precise, and understandable internal movie scenario, index the relational word. Index it in terms of degree, extent, criteria, etc.

"I've never been more depressed." *On a scale from 1 to 10, how depressed have you ever felt? What degree of these down-feelings have you experienced before? What facets of your thinking-feeling, behaving, etc. have you depressed?*

Sometimes **what** a person deletes or fails to specify concerns the standards by which they make comparisons. "She's the best cook." This model suggests that we respond to *such unspecified relations* by indexing the comparative standard that the person has deleted. *Best in what way, under what circumstances, at what time?* "He's better at golf." *Better than whom?*

4. Unspecified Processes—Adjectives Modifying Nouns
Bandler and Grinder added another form of deletion to the Meta-model that has itself become deleted in most current versions of the Meta-model. They explained their reasoning in this way:

> *"One of the ways in which Deep Structure process words may occur in Surface Structure is in the form of an adjective which modifies a noun. In order for this to happen, deletions must occur."* (p. 62)

Thus in the expression, *I don't like unclear people*, we have the adjective *unclear*, yet the speaker has deleted the context, "unclear to whom, about what, when, etc.?" So with other examples:
   a. *I laughed at the irritating man.*
   b. *You always present stupid examples.*
   c. *The unhappy letter surprised me.*

In these cases where a speaker has deleted the process of accessing a state of consciousness characterized by "lack of clarity," "irritation," "stupidity," and "unhappiness," not only has the process become solidified in a trait label, but the speaker has projected it out from him or herself to the stimulus. Thus we have a man who in some way provided some stimulus to which the speaker thinks-and-feels irritated (first process). The speaker then projects his or her thoughts-and-feelings of irritation to the man and labels him with his state (second process).

As an aside, this languaging actually indicates a meta-level process. The evaluations (irritating, stupid, unhappy) occur at a level *above* the referent (man, examples, letter). It therefore designates the speaker's *meta-state* from which he or she projects and imposes their model onto the world. I have detailed the NLP Meta-States model in several works (Hall, 1995, 1996, 1997).

5. Unspecified Processes—Adverbs Modifying Verbs
Here we have a process hidden by the use of an adverb that typically ends in *ly*. In other words, the *ly* adverb deletes the process and solidifies the result by applying a "state" word (word indicating a state of mind-body consciousness) to a verb.

> *Unfortunately, you forgot to call me on my birthday.*
> *I quickly left the argument.*
> *Surprisingly, my father lied about his drinking.*
> *She slowly started to cry.*

The Meta-model procedure for recovering the deleted material involves putting the phrase *"It is..."* in front of the former adverb.

> *It is unfortunate that you forgot to call me on my birthday.*
> *It is quick that I left the argument.*
> *It is surprising my father lied about his drinking.*
> *It is slow that she started to cry.*

This reveals the modifier of the action (or verb) as a process itself—a quality or characteristic of the person's state: sometimes a mental judgment (unfortunately), sometimes a way of doing something (quickly, slowly), a state of mind (surprisingly), etc.

Linguistic Generalizations

6. **Universal Quantifiers (UQ)**
7. **Modal Operators (MO)**
8. **Lost Performatives (LP)**

When we make generalizations, we take elements or pieces of an experience and we let them *represent an entire category.* Such generalizing occurs due to the way our sense receptors and nervous system relate to the energy manifestations *out there.* We generalize to reduce the world to more manageable proportions. Yet because this modeling frequently leaves us with impoverished maps, we need to constantly run checks on our generalizing. *Does this generalization make life more productive and empowering?* By generalizing we create our rules and programs for living, relating, communicating, etc.

Generalizations often outlive their usefulness. The following rules may have proved useful for a kid in a dysfunctional home, but may have lost their usefulness for adult life. "Don't express feelings." "Don't disagree with dad." "Don't point out incongruencies in parents." "Be seen, but not heard." This underscores the importance of continually checking our maps and re-evaluating generalizations.

Under *generalization,* the Meta-model specifies structures that we commonly use to create rules, classes, classifications, and abstractions that can impoverish our lives. Though we inevitably create and use generalizations to cope, they frequently impoverish by causing a loss of detail and richness. This leaves us without the ability to make the necessary distinctions. When we generalize, we leave characteristics out (deletion) as we form abstractions that summarize our learnings.

"I can't trust people." "It's no fun to learn." "Change is hard." "Things should be easier." Such generalized statements carry no specific referential index. Thus the abstraction carries no time-index (when), person-index (who), place-index (where), context index (under what circumstances), etc. This invites us to treat them as absolutes and universals. Yet if we do, we thereby turn them into insidious and dangerous maps.

To challenge this ill-formedness, require the speaker to supply the referential indices.

> *"Who, specifically?"*
> *"Specifically when, where, under what circumstances?"*

6. Universal Quantifiers refer to generalizing a whole class in terms of *allness*. We code universal quantifiers in words that describe things in *all or nothing terms* (all, every, none, everybody, always, totally, absolutely, etc.) With these words we over-generalize experience. *"Nobody* pays any attention to me." *"Everybody* hates me." "Why do I *always* get the bum deal?"

When we generalize we create an abstract map in a global way; we quantify our statements with the universal terms. This All-or-Nothing language represents what Korzybski called "one valued" or "two valued" abstractions. It creates a polarization of thought-and-emotion and, more typically than not, mis-maps the world inasmuch as it completely overlooks that most things occur in steps, stages, and along a continuum.

> "Nobody pays any attention to what I say."
> "I always avoid situations where I feel uncomfortable."

To challenge global maps of universals, directly question them. *"Nobody has ever paid even the least bit of attention to you?"* This response runs with the exaggeration in the map, and highlights the exaggeration. Simultaneously, it calls for the person to consider exceptions to the generalization.

> *"A single exception to the generalization starts the client on the process of assigning referential indices and insures the detail and richness in the client's model necessary to have a variety of options for coping."* (p. 83)

Many statements occur that only *imply universalization* and do not actually state such. "You just can't trust people." *"Nobody? A person can't trust another single human being?" "Have you ever trusted anyone?" "Suppose you allow yourself to imagine a circum-*

stance in which you could trust someone?" Again, such questions invite the speaker to re-examine the map, to reconnect it to experience, and to look for counter-examples that call it in question. These questions also encourage a new re-mapping.

Bandler and Grinder also suggested another response—"counter-exampling." This relativizes the generalization from a mere abstraction and connects it to *immediate* experience. *"Do you trust me right now in this situation?" "So should I not trust you in this situation right now?"* I shall explain these "Sleight of Mouth" patterns more fully in Chapter Six.

Once we have found and elicited a counter-example to the over-generalization, this begins to deframe the old belief statement. Now we can explore differences. Doing a *contrastive analysis* between two experiences then enables us to identify specifically *the difference* that makes a difference. *"What differs between the person or persons who can trust or have trusted and the ones who cannot?" "What stops you from trusting someone?" "What would happen if you did trust someone?" "What would allow you to trust them?"*

7. Modal Operators refer to those *"modes"* in which one *operates* in the world. We may characterize these "modes of operating" in terms of **necessity, desire, possibility, impossibility,** etc. Such terms delete the rules or generalizations in one's model.

These words indicate a person's *mode* or *state* and so identify a conceptual state from which the person operates. As "modal operators," therefore they indicate *our "mode" of response.* Some "modes" from which we "operate" create limitations for us. They generate a conceptual state that limits our sense of choice and/or that transforms the kind of "reality" we experience. Responding effectively to such "state words" by breaking down those general-izations enables us to expand our boundaries and depotentate (to use Erickson's terminology) limitations.

"I have to think about others' feelings."
"I can't stand criticism."

As we delete and leave characteristics out, we then create rules or generalizations. These create various *modi operandi* for functioning in the world. We generate these *operational styles* in our mental maps, in fact, by using special kind of words—Modal Operators. I "have to, must, need to," etc. Such words describe the operational mode of *necessity*. Other operational modes also exist: *possibility* ("can, may, want to, get to, can"), *impossibility* ("can't, not possible, may not," etc.).

"I have to (must, need to) consider the feelings of others."

For the modal operators of necessity, the speaker has deleted the consequence."*Or what?*" "*What will happen if you don't?*" For the modal operators of impossibility, the speaker has deleted the inhibiting forces. "*What makes this impossible?*" "*What stops you?*" (or use "prevents," "blocks," "inhibits").

Now since we know that "trusting people" exists as a possibility for some humans, then we know "that the world is rich enough to allow the client to come to trust people—it's that person's model which prevents it." So we ask,

"What stops you from trusting people?"
"What would happen if you trusted a person?"

As the person answers, he or she begins to restore deleted material, thereby producing a clearer map, and re-connecting it to the experiences from which they created their map. Then to expand their map and to begin to identify needed resources, we can shift the referential index.

"Do you know anyone who can trust people?"

"Can you imagine someone trusting people safely and with confidence?"

"What allows them to do that?"

8. Lost Performatives (Unspecified Speakers or Map-Makers) refer to evaluative statements in the form of generalizations about the world, people, life, etc. These evaluative statements usually involve *an un-owned judgment*. The one who performed the evaluating has deleted him or herself from the statement. The result? A definitive map-statement about reality, but no map-maker who performed this operation.

Lost Performatives function as *rules* for life made up by someone. Yet inasmuch as the performer has excluded him or herself from the statement, they not only do not take responsibility for the map they offer, but further present it as universally applicable as an absolute "truth." And because these Lost Performatives generally sound like mandates from heaven, they invite us to step into "the deity mode" in our thinking and speaking! "Boys shouldn't cry." "Don't talk about yourself; it'll go to your head and people won't like you."

When we consider the indexing question of *who performs* the action of mapping out their construction of reality in a certain way—we ask about the speaker of a generalization. But when we delete the performer ("performative" in transformational grammar), then we have a surface expression "not relativized" to the speaker. For example, "It's wrong to hurt someone's feelings."

> *"There is no indication in the Surface Structure that the client is aware that the statement made is true for his particular model; that there is no indication that the client recognizes that there may be other possibilities."* (p. 106)

By challenging this mapping generalization, by asking "according to whom?" "according to whom at what point in time?" we recover the generalization or rule and so that the person can "see these generalizations as true for his belief system at a specific moment in time" (p. 107).

> "It's bad to be inconsistent."
> *Who said that? Upon what did the speaker base the criteria of 'badness? 'How do you know that we should evaluate it as bad?*

Here we have a statement but no speaker—a linguistic observation (or map) but no observer (map-maker). Someone has deleted *the performer* of the map which leaves us with no information about the map-maker. All that remains involves only a generalized "rule" of reality which leaves the impression that it stands as **an absolute truth for all times, places, people, etc.**

We bring a touch of sanity to such unspecified speaker statements by indexing these concerns: "We all know that it's wrong to slow the group down." *Who says this? Wrong in what way or for whom?* "He's acting funny." *Who believes that he is acting in a funny way?*

Linguistic Distortions

9. *Nominalization* (Nom.)
10. *Mind-Reading* (MR)
11. *Cause-Effect* (C-E)
12. *Complex Equivalences* (CEq.)
13. *Presuppositions* (Ps.)

When we distort experience we make shifts in how we represent/experience sensory data. In fantasy, we distort information to plan, rehearse, create, and imagine a wide range of possibilities. This can powerfully enrich our world as it can also limit the richness of reality. It all depends upon context and intent. Distortion can discount a loving affirmation, "She just says that because she wants something." It can create good feelings in response to "negative" events, "I learned so many wonderful things through that accident (divorce, bankruptcy)." Under this category of *distortion*, we will find linguistic expressions that altered or changed a representation.

9. Nominalizations refer to *giving names* to describe actions or ongoing events with the result that the speaker turns verbs and predicates into static entities (nouns). This **nominalizing** of ongoing processes turns them into "things," entities, and fixed/finished processes. Doing this creates a model of the world as fixed, static, unmoving, permanent, and finished. It then becomes easy to believe that one can do nothing about it, that change cannot occur, that one has no power to make things better, etc. When we do this about processes, this truly generates a model that most find limiting, impoverishing, and victimizing. In nominalizing, we delete the action and process of the territory and create a highly distorted map.

The linguistic process of nominalization involves a complex transformational process whereby a process word or verb in the Deep Structure appears as a finished and static thing in the Surface Structure. Here an ongoing process or event gets transformed into a static thing; a verb turns into a noun.

Suzette Elgin (1980) has described these pseudo-nouns as "verby things turned into nouny things." They actually exist and operate as *hidden verbs.*

This distortion can powerfully impoverish a cognitive map inasmuch as the person comes to assume something as fixed and frozen in reality and beyond his or her influence. The "deciding" becomes a "decision." By recovering facets left out and reordering one's structure of the phenomenon (turning a static thing back into an ongoing process), this enriches one's map.

> *"Reversing nominalizations assists the client in coming to see that what he had considered an event, finished and beyond his control, is an ongoing process which can be changed."* (p. 74)

To test for a nominalization, check to see if the noun will fit into the linguistic phrase, *"an ongoing ..."*. True nouns indicating a person, place, or thing will not. Pseudo-nouns indicating processes will fit. "An ongoing door" (lamp, kite, book) doesn't seem well-formed, whereas "An ongoing decision" (marriage, failure, motivation) does. Use this syntactic frame to test words that sound like, look like, and feel like concrete things, but actually hide a verb and process underneath the noun-like garb.

> "My divorce is painful."
> *"The experience of divorcing gave me a lot of pain." "I experienced a lot of pain when I divorced my spouse."*

> "Our terror blocks us."
> *"Thinking-and-feeling in exaggerated fear terms blocks us."*

"Your perception is seriously wrong."
"How you perceive the situation contains some important errors..."

"My confusion has a tendency to give me no relief."
"When I fuse the several factors together, I then tend to create an experience within which I cannot relieve myself of emotional distress."

The Meta-model offers a second test for nominalizations—*the wheelbarrow test.* Can you put (or imagine putting) the referent of the word in a wheelbarrow? We can put true nouns that refer to tangible "things" into a wheelbarrow or on a table. We cannot, however, so put the pseudo-nouns. They do not have such tangibility inasmuch as they consist of ongoing processes.

Form a visual image from the sentence. Then see if you can imagine placing the referent of the non-process word in it.

To challenge the ill-formedness of a nominalization, we can directly question its supposed "concreteness."

"I regret my decision."
"What if you decided to think again and alter what you first decided?"
"What stops you from changing the decision?"

In the statement, "I can't stand her insensitivity," *insensitivity* can not fit into a wheelbarrow, but it does make sense if we say, "an ongoing insensitivity." To de-nominalize, we need only explore the hidden verb. *Her not sensing what? And about whom? Sensing how specifically?*

As we **de-nominalize**, we *identify the hidden process* within the so-called noun and explicate the workings of that process.

"Frustration"—*Who or what frustrates whom?*
"Happiness"—*Who feels happy about what?*
"Productivity"—*Who produces what?*
"Relationship"—*Who relates to whom, and how, and when, and under what conditions?*
"Skill level"—*Who demonstrates skills, toward what subject?*
"There's a lot of tension there."—*Who tenses their muscles about what?*

Some nominalizations seem especially insidious due to their vagueness and their removal from the underlying verb by arising from another language. When such troublesome nominalizations strike our consciousness, we do not detect the process representation at all. For instance:

> **Wind**: *How does the air move?*
> **Mind**: *What or how do you entertain thought?*
> **Religion**: (from Latin, "to bind back"). *What do you value as having great importance to you? To whom or what does your belief bind you back to? How?*
> **Self-esteem**: *In what way do you value yourself? According to what standard?*
> **Pain**: *What hurts? Where?*

Poetically, in nominalization, we take *frog-in-process* and knight it with a magic wand that transforms it into *a princely-noun*. This provides a significant challenge to clarity. Once these noun-ified verbs put on royal robes and stand around presenting a cold, superior lordly stare, and do not leap about (like true frogs always in action), it becomes difficult to tell *what* these words *refer to*, or how their symbolism should work in terms of our mental representations.

These nounified words look like and sound like *"things."* **Reification**, from the verb "to reify," comes from the Latin word "res" which refers to a "thing." Hence, "to regard an abstraction (concept, idea) as if a material thing."

In terms of clarity and sanity, when we use nominalizations we send very *false signals to our brain*. We send messages with a different structure from the territory. The linguistic coding cues us to think-feel and respond to the referent as to a solid, stable, static-like thing rather than a process of movement and fluidity. We cannot put the referent of the so-called "noun" in a wheel-barrow or on a table. If we could, the process would not stay there, but move and leap and jump.

Nominalizations as *mental abstractions of verbs* have lost specificity about their movements. They not only send poor signals to the brain about processes, but deceptive messages. As linguistic structures, nominalizations operate as impostures. Though dressed up as nouns, they mask an underlying verb process.

To keep one's mental screen clean, we need to **de-nominalize.** We have to find and re-language the hidden verb. This makes the frog appear underneath all the royal dress-up. This transforms the static structure allowing us to see the underlying action. In this way we linguistically arrest the nominalization, disrobe it, strip-search it, and discover the process beneath the cover-up.

We nominalize by giving names to processes comprised of higher level mental abstractions so that we name things which do not truly exist as "things." We create such names as: "good," "bad," "no," "love," "God." These words serve as symbols for *intangible referents* like ideas, experiences, and non-corporal beings. In **denominalizing**, we identify the nounified process words as pseudo-nouns, recover the hidden verb, and then treat the verb as we would any other unspecific verb.

> "Let's improve our communication so that our relationship will give us more satisfaction."
> *How do we **communicate** with each other now? How would you like to **communicate**? What facet of our **sending messages back and forth** in an exchange seems to need improving?*

Such denominalizing empowers us by enabling us to reconnect to the processes. When we do not challenge nominalizations, the structure of this process word implies a static and permanent reality. Nominalizations signal the brain no movement or action. This implies permanence, no change, unchangeable, hence stuck, etc. Turn the words back into verbs to recover a sense of movement, choice, and clarity.

When we endow our labels and concepts with a kind of concreteness ("misplaced concreteness," Bertrand Russell, 1910), we thereafter begin to feel and behave according to that map. As this delusion continues, we begin to respond as if others will equally see and share our attributes about things. To the extent that they do, we experience shared conceptual "reality."

10. Mind-Reading. In mind-reading, we make a statement that claims or assumes knowledge of the internal state of another person (their thoughts, emotions, values, intentions, etc.). We do so without having received direct communication from the person or we do so without specifying the process whereby we attained such knowledge. Mind-reading statements consist of a combination of presuppositions, deletions, and referential index shifts. These often indicate feel-see, feel-hear synesthesia patterns—cross-sensory patterns.

The semantic ill-formedness here involves the speaker's belief that he or she knows the internal state, mind, emotions, intentions, etc. of another person without direct communication. "Everybody in the groups thinks I'm stupid." These expressions presuppose that the person can directly read the minds of others or can jump to such conclusions based on various non-verbal expressions. The distorted structure occurs due to the speaker first deleting the process of *how* he or she knows the mind of another and then to failing to make the guesses tentative. Failing to do this prevents the speaker from *checking out* his or her guesses by inviting the other to provide a clarification.

Cause-effect expressions limit choices by presupposing that some cause outside of oneself "makes" or "forces" one to have this or that experience. Mind-reading expressions limit choices by assuming one already knows what another thinks-and-feels. If we make this assumption, we won't bother to inquire about another's thoughts, feelings, values, etc. People who mind-read a lot tend not to express their own thoughts and feelings and may further even expect others to "just know" what they think-and-feel.

The concern here does not lie in the question of whether human beings can read, or can learn to read, the minds-and-emotions of others. Such phenomena may indeed occur. Yet the fact that most of us have a difficult enough time reading our own thoughts-and-emotions, intentions, and motives, etc. ought to warn us against assuming too much in this area. Further, the fact that "the source of vast amounts of inter-personal difficulties, miscommunication and its accompanying pain" (p. 105) arises from mind-reading should caution us to go slow in this area.

To challenge or question mind-reading, we index the *how do you know*.

> *How do you know that everybody thinks this about you?*
> *How do you know that John feels disgusted with you?*
> *How specifically does this process occur and how do you know this?*

> "Susan never considers my feelings!"
> *How do you know that Susan does not consider your feelings?*

> "You have lost respect for our president!"
> *What behaviors or words gives you the impression that I have shifted my feelings of respect regarding the president?*

As we live with others and relate to them, then over time we do pick up on each other's patterns as we *become more calibrated* to each other's style, states, and orientation. Consequently, the longer people relate, the more frequently and naturally people fall into mind-reading patterns. This does not necessarily indicate a bad thing or a dysfunction. Again, it depends entirely upon the condition and quality of a couple's relatings. Mind-reading that does not allow for each person to have the last word about their own state holds much potential for harm.

When people become calibrated to each other and do not "pace" each other's values, principles, visions, understandings, beliefs, etc. they will tend to use hurtful and conflictual languaging. Each will attempt to *tell* the other what the other *really* means and intends! Mind-reading becomes especially prevalent in the communication pattern of "crazymaking." This pattern can drive people bananas.

Mind-reading differs from Lost Performatives in that this languaging identifies or describes internal states. By contrast, lost performatives pass judgments. Hence, "You should be a man and not cry!" indicates a lost performative. "You're trying to hurt my feelings" indicates mind-reading.

Inaccurate mind-reading statements feel insulting, intrusive, foreign, and "controlling." People who receive such will typically go into states of feeling misunderstood, invisible, controlled, invaded, etc. On other occasions, inaccurate mind-reading statements will elicit an energized state wherein someone attempts to explain his or her true feelings and to assert his or her truths. Typically they will do this in a defensive way.

Inaccurate mind-reading statements by parents, teachers or other adults often evoke in children a distrust of their own consciousness as they accept the foreign attributions. If the child retains consciousness of this, they may feel caught between two conflicting messages. This kind of "crazymaking" may then cause a splitting off of the self in order to cope with the double messages (Bateson, 1972).

Accurate mind-reading statements, conversely, can sometimes enable a person to discover his or her thoughts, motives, etc. and feel validated. Gentle, tentative mind-reading often occurs in therapy as an essential part of the healing. The therapist's "reading" of the client's mind, motives, intentions, desires, etc. and articulation aims to communicate a validation and acceptance. Yet, depending upon how the client "reads" this—this can also backfire. Therefore the need arises for the therapist to do it with gentleness and tentativeness—letting the client ultimately accept, temper or reject the mind-reading statements.

11. Cause-Effect. These statements assert that one thing *necessarily causes* another thing. These statements indicate beliefs and presuppositions about causation. We usually find these encoded with unspecified causal verbs (e. g. "make," "cause," "force," etc.) or almost any active verb. Such language suggests a linkage between a stimulus and a response which may not actually exist as directly or logically connected.

Typically we distort things by the way we assign "cause." This becomes especially true when we assign causation that belongs to us (things we can do, response-abilities we do have) to sources outside of ourselves. The statement, "Jim makes me angry." fits this description as does, "George forced Mary to weigh 175 pounds."

> *"Some person causes some person to have some emotion. When the first person, the one doing the causing, is different from the person experiencing the anger, the sentence is said to be semantically ill-formed and unaccepted. The semantic ill-formedness of sentences of this type arises because it, literally, is not possible for one human being to create an emotion in another human being.... [Actually] ... the emotion is a response generated from a model in which the client takes no responsibility for experiences which he could control."* (pp. 51-52)

Although the two events (the causing and the result) occur one after another, we do not necessarily have "causation" occurring here, only some relationship or correlation. How can we challenge the model to empower the person to take responsibility for his or her own responses? We can ask such questions as:

> Does Jim *always* make you feel angry when he does that?
> Has there *ever* been a time when you didn't respond with anger to that?
> Do you *have to* feel anger at that?
> What *forces* you to feel anger at that?
> What difference explains why sometimes you feel anger and sometimes you don't?

We have a clear image of someone's model when we see their behaviors, talk, and emotions as *making sense* given that map. Until then, we do not truly understand the person.

This form of semantic ill-formedness leads to limitations inasmuch as it creates a map of the world wherein the person represents him or herself as having no choice in responding as he or she does. *Implied causation* typically shows up simply in direct active tense verbs. "She depresses me." This has the same meaning (at the Deep Structure of transformational grammar) as:

"She makes me feel depressed."
"You bore me"—"You make me feel bored."

"She makes me angry" represents a vague image in which one person performs an action whereby another person experiences some inner state of thought or emotion (anger).
How specifically does she 'make' you angry?
Does her action always operate to create this effect in you?
Has she ever performed that action and you have not responded with anger?

Cause-effect statements frequently identify synesthesia patterns like see-feel and hear-feel circuits. "These ideas make me excited." *How specifically do you experience excitement in response to those ideas?* Statements that make predictions about the future contain cause-effect statements. "You'll never be happy with him!" "Will never be" codes causation. Since cause-effect statements identify how things work, or what controls what, concepts of responsibility frequently get tied up with this pattern.

Implied causation can show up using various causation words ("that," "since," "because"). "I'm sad that you forgot our anniversary" (substitute "since," "because," "inasmuch," etc.). Causation ideas can also hide beneath the cue word *but*. Here one may use the word "but" to reference his or her reasons and conditions that cause their situation. "I want to leave home, but my father is sick." The father being sick makes or causes the person to experience the inability to leave home.

"I don't want to get angry, but she is always blaming me."
"I don't enjoy being uptight, but my job demands it."

In response to these cause-effect statements, we can enrich the person's model and his or her sense of choice by questioning the universality of the statement. *"Do you always get mad when she blames?"* We can ask for more specificity. *"How specifically does her blaming make you feel angry?"* We can inquire more about the cause-effect relationship. *"If she didn't blame you, you would not get angry at her?"*

In the Meta-model a "special kind of deletion" occurs in sentences that map out causation—when the causation involves a system of inter-actions, but the expressions only detail one side. In addition to the *universals* ("always," "never") in the following lines, we have an incomplete model of an inter-action.

"My husband is always arguing with me."
"My wife never smiles at me."

Bandler and Grinder write,

"The image of the processes or relationships of arguing with and smiling at are incomplete as only one person in the relationship is being describes as having an active role. When faced with Surface Structures of this type, the therapist has the choice of asking for the way the person characterized as passive is involved in the process." (p. 85)

This *cause-effect deletion* now brings up another important linguistic distinction. This comes from Bateson's (1972) work with symmetry. Bateson noted that in relationships, we can have symmetrical and non-symmetrical relations. Symmetrically, if "I am your peer," then of necessity, "you are my peer." But non-symmetrically, if "I am your father," the converse cannot also hold true. If, "I am your brother," you may or may not "be a brother" to me, you may be a sister.

The words "argue with" indicate a symmetrical relationship. If I "argue with" you, then of necessity this implies that you "argue with" me. After all, as we commonly say, "It takes two to argue." With symmetrical predicates, the Meta-model suggests that we *shift referential indices.* "Then you also argue a lot with your husband?"

We can illustrate a non-symmetrical predicate with the other example, "smile at." Here it does not take two to smile. So logically, while one person may never smile at another, the other may smile, may even typically smile at the first one. Yet psychologically while no logical necessity demands it,

"...our experience has been that the converse is frequently psychologically accurate. Often the client states a generalization about another person ... the converse is true." (p. 87)

12. Complex Equivalences. These refer to a complex generalization wherein a person claims that something *means or equates to* something else. Hence, two experiences come to stand for each other which may not exist as necessarily synonymous. "He doesn't appreciate me; he never smiles at me."

The complexity of these equivalences does not lie in their structure; in structure they have a simple form: *"This = That"* (X = Y). The complexity arises from *the thinking* that produces the equation. By paying attention to how we make equivalences, we can learn a great deal about how people construct beliefs out of their generalizations.

When we equate two things that differ and that do not exist as synonyms of the same phenomenon, then we create a complex equivalence. Typically, this involves two phenomena that do not even exist on the same logical level as when we equate an externally verifiable experience ("she doesn't smile at me") with *a meaning attribution* of an internal state ("she doesn't appreciate me"). The first description allows us to empirically test it by using our senses. The second evaluation phrase does not. The second refers to a higher level of abstraction and results from the person having constructed a significance that he or she has attached to the external stimuli.

We can challenge each of these generalizations individually in terms of unspecified nouns, verbs, relations, etc. Or, if we want to use a short-cut technique we can question the overall construction. Typically this generates some dramatic results. The Meta-model describes the form of the logic in a complex equivalence in the equation: X = Y where X stands for the external behavior (EB) and Y stands for the internal state (IS). Thus:

"When she doesn't smile at me (EB), I know she doesn't appreciate me (IS)."

We can question this formulation (this constructed reality) by shifting referential indices again.

"When you don't smile at him, does that mean that you don't appreciate him?"

Or we could directly question and challenge the belief statement,

> *"Does his not smiling at you always mean the lack of appreciation?"*
> *"What experiences in your learning history has led you to draw this conclusion?"*

13. Presuppositions. These refer to those ideas and beliefs that we *assume* from the beginning. A presupposition consists of those things that must *exist as true* in order for a statement to make sense. They refer back to the paradigmatic assumptions about reality, truth, knowledge, being, personality, etc. that we hold to without questioning. By etymological definition a presupposition refers to "what comes before" (pre) "that holds our statements, understandings, and/or beliefs" (position) "up" (sup).

Presuppositions in language contain the working (and hidden) assumptions that drive the person's model of the world.

> *"Presuppositions are what is necessarily true for the statements that the client makes to make sense (not to be true, but just to be meaningful) at all. ... Presuppositions are particularly insidious as they are not presented openly for consideration."* (p. 53)

The Meta-model suggests that we identify the basic assumptions that impoverish our model to expose it for the limitations that it creates. Asking ourselves what has to "exist as true" in order for a statement to make sense enables us to flush out presuppositions. Frequently these hide as descriptions or clauses within statements.

> "I'm afraid that my son is turning out to be as lazy as my husband."

While the description here (of laziness) **sets the frame** of the mother's perception, she expresses it here as an assumption and so never explicitly presents it. A great many *syntactic environments* facilitate the presence of presuppositions. Any statement that follows main verbs like *realize, aware, ignore,* etc. frames a presupposition. Bandler and Grinder provided a list of 36 syntactic environments for presuppositions in their original work in Appendix B. "*Since* you understand this so quickly, we can go ahead with some illustrations"—everything after the word "since" in this first clause comes presupposed.

Once detected we can then simply question or challenge the presuppositional frames-of-reference that we hear. "How specifically do you know that your son or your husband acts lazily?"

To flush out presuppositions we can use several sentence completion forms. We can use the syntactic stems: *"There exists..."* and *"It stands as possible that..."* With any sentence offered we can examine the presuppositions by utilizing these sentence stems. Presuppositions indicates a person's basic reality organizing principles.

Korzybski used another phrase for presuppositions. Describing them as *undefined terms,* he said that we need to recognize our undefined terms as such. The reason? Because by means of them we assume all kinds of ideas and concepts that make up our epistemological and ontological beliefs. If we do not recognize and identify the *undefined presuppositional terms* by which we operate—we will neither fully understand our map of the world nor distinguish it from the territory. Conversely, when we challenge our undefined terms, we thereby "lay on the table our metaphysics and our assumed structures" (1933: 155). Korzybski also called these presuppositions "heavy terms" (p. liv) inasmuch as others have loaded them with meaning.

There you have it—**13 distinctions in neuro-linguistic mapping**. These 13 distinctions highlight mapping processes—which in themselves operate neutrally, hence exist as neither good nor bad. Yet in various contexts and given contextual outcomes and criteria, we can use them to create limitations, inhibitions, dysfunctions, and problems. When we so use them, we can generate very unenhancing maps that then prevent us from getting to and using our resources.

Significantly, we have numerous *linguistic markers* that cue us about these mapping distinctions. We can use these to sound the alarm that a potential mapping problem of fuzziness, deletion, or corruption has occurred. Seeing and hearing these warning signals (i. e. the linguistic markers) empowers us to notice the mapping, check for productivity, and enrich the map when necessary.

In a word, this describes the function and usefulness of the Meta-model. It enables us to take a meta-position to our cognitive maps and check them out for usefulness, accuracy, and desirability. If we then discover a particular restrictiveness in one of our maps that causes us pain or that prevents us from living more resourcefully, with the Meta-model we now have the insight and technology for expanding our model of the world.

The Meta-Model Strategy

The overall Meta-model *strategy* involves careful listening as people communicate in their everyday surface expressions. We then represent the words as a sensory movie and notice the missing or unclear parts. Once we have "tracked" their words over to sensory-based referents, we then can explore, question, and challenge the ill-formed statements. By doing this we recover deleted, generalized, and distorted parts of the map that impoverish the person's thinking. Doing this simultaneously invites the person to reconnect to the experience out of which his or her linguistic model came. By design we seek to elicit greater clarity, to depotentate (de-power) the person's "rules," and to assist them in building a more empowering model of the world.

We therefore talk about *"meta-modeling"* someone. This means listening and identifying language "violations to well-formedness" (e. g. cognitive maps involving vagueness, imprecision, deletions, fuzziness, and distortions) in order to challenge them. Making these challenges typically elicits a fuller and richer mental map that both allows and empowers us to live more fully.

This model also contains **a set of questions** to use in eliciting another set of statements characterized by well-formedness in structure, syntax, and semantics. Asking such questions re-activates the person's own neuro-linguistic mapping processes. It thus invites the person to become an active re-creator of his or her reality.

Chart 2:1

The Meta-Model Of Language

1. Simple Deletions
"They don't listen to me."
> *Who specifically doesn't listen to you?*

"People push me around."
> *Who specifically pushes you?*

2. Comparative And Superlative Deletions: Unspecified Relations
"She's a better person."
> *Better than whom? Better at what? Compared to whom, what? Given what criteria?*

3. Unspecified Referential Indices: Unspecified Nouns And Verbs
"I am uncomfortable."
> *Uncomfortable in what way? Uncomfortable when?*

"He said that she was mean."
> *Whom did he say that you call mean? What did he mean by 'mean'?*

"She rejected me."
> *How specifically did she reject you?*

"I felt really manipulated."
> *Manipulated in what way and how?*

4. Unspecified Processes—Adverbs Modifying Verbs
"Surprisingly, my father lied about his drinking."
> *How did you feel surprised about that? What surprised you about that?*

"She slowly started to cry."
> *What indicated to you that her starting to cry occurred in a slow manner?*

5. Unspecified Processes—Adjectives Modifying Nouns
"I don't like unclear people."
> *Unclear about what and in what way?*

"The unhappy letter surprised me."
> *How, and in what way, did you feel unhappy about the letter?*

6. Universal Quantifiers: Allness: Generalizations that exclude exceptions

> "She never listens to me."
>> *Never? She has never so much as listened to you even a little bit?*

7. Modal Operators: Operational Modes of Being—One's Modus Operandi

> "I have to take care of her."
>> *What would happen if you didn't? What wouldn't happen if you didn't? You have to or else what?*

8. Lost Performatives: Evaluative statement(s) with the speaker deleted or unowned

> "It's bad to be inconsistent."
>> *Who evaluates it as bad? According to what standard? How do you determine this label of "badness?"*

9. Nominalizations: Processes transformed into static "things."

> "Let's improve our communication."
>> *Whose communicating do you mean? How would you like to communicate?*
> "What state did you wake up in this morning?"
>> *How specifically did you think and feel when you woke up?*

10. Mind-Reading: Attributing knowledge of another's internal thoughts, feelings, motives

> "You don't like me..."
>> *How do you know I don't like you? What evidence leads you to think that?*

11. Cause-Effect: Causational statements of relations between events, stimulus-response beliefs

> "You make me sad."
>> *How does my behavior cause you to respond with sad feelings? Do you always feel sad when I do this? How specifically does this work?*

12. Complex Equivalences: Phenomena that differ which someone equates as the same

> "She's always yelling at me; she doesn't like me."
>> *How do you equate her yelling as meaning she doesn't like you? Can you recall a time when you yelled at someone that you liked?*

> "He's a loser when it comes to business, he just lacks business sense."
>> *How do you know to equate his lack of success in business with his lack of business sense? Could other factors play a role in this?*

13. Presuppositions: Silent Assumptions, Unspoken Paradigms

> "If my husband knew how much I suffered, he wouldn't do that."
>> *How do you suffer? In what way? About what? How do you know that your husband knows or doesn't know this? Why do you assume that his intentions would shift if he knew? Does your husband always use your emotional state to determine his responses?*

Language Patterns Of The Meta-Model

The *challenges* within the Meta-model simply refer to *the questions* we use to elicit higher quality information. We challenge the old mapping when we ask *what, which, when, whom and how* questions.

This model at this point does **not** ask *why* questions. *Why questions* do not produce much value in terms of gathering high quality information while working within the old frames. Why questions evoke explanations, reasons, history, rationalizations, excuses, defensiveness, etc. Why questions also do not get specific details, but "becauses..." Here we want *process* information: how, when, where, for whom, what, which, etc.

[Why questions in the context of exploring meta-levels about values—the why of importance—does play a crucial role in value elicitation. "Why do you find that important?" "Why does that mean so much to you?" Likewise, the why of teleology works wonders in eliciting desired outcomes. "Why do you want to do this?" "What will you get from it?" But the why of source or origin (while a person still lives, perceives, thinks, feels, and operates under the old frame) typically only reinforces the generalizations and justifies them.]

The Meta-model provides a technology for asking the best kind of questions for drawing out and actively engaging the speaker. Inasmuch as this model starts from the assumption that our languaging suffers from incomplete, fuzzy, and unclear representations, the questions function as a de-fuzzy-ing process. By them we gather high quality responses for more clarity, specificity, and precision.

Jacobson (1986) asserted that the Meta-model provides "a great set of rules to guide your thinking."

"Remember that language is a reflection of what is in our minds. If our words come out like a tossed salad, well...So listen to your language when you talk with people..." (p. 106)

We can use the Meta-model to guide our thinking. To do so, let it order, sequence, and structure your thinking in more productive ways. As these patterns of questions become habitual, you will automatically think, "When and where would this behavior naturally occur?" "What stimulus has elicited this response?" "What does this statement imply about the person's meanings?" etc.

Dilts (1983) has described the Meta-model in terms of *an explicit set of questions and a model for asking questions* (pp. 77-79). The Meta-model responses also include **meta-questions**. These enable us to step back from the entire mapping process as we inquire about *the form and structure* of a person's languaging and to look at the mapping processes to check out the person's deleting of possibly critical information and his or her style and manner of generalizing and distorting.

Using these questions enables us as listeners to *stay in sensory awareness* in gathering information. It empowers us **from** going inside and internally generating our own experience and meanings rather than getting the speaker's understanding. In the place where we might have previously made reference to our own experiences (e. g. "I know what you mean, why back in 1983, I had a similar experience..."), we can now use the Meta-model questions. In facilitating people to make their communications clearer, we will no longer fill in the pieces from our own model. "Filling in the pieces" with our own map means we meet the other person at our model of the world. The Meta-model helps us to avoid that. Now we can meet the other person **at his or her model of the world**.

Conclusion

Though we live in a real external world, we do not operate directly or immediately upon that world. We operate indirectly through a map that guides our behaviors and responses. These maps necessarily differ from the territory they model by three processes: generalization, deletion, and distortion. A model of our model provides a representation for thinking about our languaging. The NLP Meta-model of language goes further. It provides a way to not only identify the structure, syntax, meaning, and value of our languaging, but it provides a user-friendly application of how to transform linguistic representations. We no longer have to feel stuck with "stinky thinking," vagueness, thinking distortions, or other forms of poor mapping.

With these thirteen linguistic distinctions and responses, we have a way to think about the Meta-modeling that occurs in "therapy." A client shows up feeling limited. He or she feels pain, distress, dissatisfaction, blocked, stuck, confused, etc. The problem does not lie in the world. There exists enough richness in the world for all kinds of fulfilling human experiences. The problem lies in the map the client uses to navigate that territory. As the therapist and client talk about these experiences and understandings, something shifts in the client's model of the world—their *representations*. With the shifting of their model, neurology changes as does "personality," "identity," emotions, behaviors, and life itself. Magic occurs.

Meta-Model Exercises

The following provides exercises that you can use to train your intuitions about the Meta-model distinctions and challenges.

Meta-modeling Limiting Beliefs
1. In groups of 3 or 4 persons.
2. Begin with the invitation for the experiencer, "As you think about some area in life in which you experience a limitation of some sort—begin to describe it for us."
3. Designate one person to serve as *recorder* to keep track of the conversation.
4. After the experiencer presents 2 or 3 minutes of information, the other members of the group should begin to *meta-model* the statements—*only* using Meta-model distinctions and questions. Especially list for nominalizations, cause-effect statements, and complex equivalences.
5. Afterwards use the *record* to check the distinctions identified and the questions used.

Beginning Meta-modeling
1. In groups of 3 or 4 persons.
2. Each person begins by making a list of 6 to 12 examples (each) of: deletions, comparative deletions, unspecified nouns, unspecified verbs, and nominalizations.
3. When ready, take turns delivering the ill-formed presentations to the others in the group—so that the group gets the experience of *meta-modeling* (asking the challenges to the statements).
4. Debrief quickly at the end of each speaker about what questions seemed most effective in gathering the highest quality information.

More Advanced Meta-modeling
1. In groups of 3 or 4 persons.
2. Each person begins by making a list of 6 to 12 examples (each) of: mind-reading, complex equivalences, modal operators, cause-effect statements, and nominalizations.
3. When ready, take turns delivering the ill-formed presentations to the others in the group—so that the group gets the experience of *meta-modeling* (asking the challenges to the statements).
4. Debrief quickly at the end of each speaker about what questions seemed most effective in gathering the highest quality information.

Finding And Exposing Psychological "Can'ts"
1. In groups of 3 or 4 persons.
2. Each person begins by completing the following *sentence stems* with a list of 6 to 12 responses:
    "I can't stand ...."
    "What really gets me and rattles my cage is...."
    "I feel most unresourceful when..."
3. Taking turns, have each person read one of his or her responses, for example, "I can't stand it when someone talks to me with a harsh tonality."
4. To this let one or more of the group members respond with appropriate *meta-modeling challenges*. For example, "What stops you from standing the other person's harsh tonality?" "What would happen if you did 'stand' that person's unpleasant tonality?"

Playing With Modals
1. In groups of 3 or 4 persons.
2. Begin with the invitation for the experiencer, "Think about some area in life in which you tell yourself that you 'have to' or 'must' do something. What do you specifically say?" (Or what do you use these words for when communicating to someone else?)

3. After the experiencer presents the information, let the other members of the group take turns *meta-modeling* him or her by shifting to other modal operators. For example, "And what would it feel like (seem like, be like) for you if you said, 'and I *get to*?'"

4. Playfully keep shifting the *modal operators* and then afterward reflect on how playing with them shifts your sense of your *modus operandi* in the world if you used them to navigate through life.

Playing With Causation

1. In groups of 3 or 4 persons.

2. As a group construct a list of *causation words* and fit them into a hierarchy that moves from "0" causation (chance, chaos, random) up the scale to more and more direct causation so that at "100" you have such conceptual terminology as "determines, makes, causes," etc. Use a sheet of paper with a Vertical Line so that the bottom represents "0" and the top represents "100."

3. Taking turns, invite the first experiencer to make a cause-effect statement that seems to create limitations for them in life. For example, "When my wife asks me to do some chore around the house, I feel manipulated."

4. Group members should first *reformulate* the statement so that it has a cause-effect format. For example, "So her asking *makes* you feel manipulated?"

5. Group members should then respond with *meta-modeling* questions and challenges that invites the experiencer to try on more or less intense causational words. For example, "How would it feel to you if her asking *invited* you to feel that way—knowing that you can always accept or reject the invitation?" "How would it feel if her asking *suggested* manipulation?"

6. Continue to enjoy the process of experiencing different levels of causational terms as each person takes a turn—and by reflecting on what works best and what has the least impact.

Meta-modeling Complex Equivalence
1. In groups of 3 or 4 persons.
2. Begin by inviting the first experiencer to present some complex equivalence that doesn't serve them well in life (a negative association or anchor that evokes an unresourceful state). For example, "When I think about someone talking to me and pointing at me with their index finger, I feel put down or scolded."
3. Group members should first confirm the complex equivalence. For example, "So, for you, a pointing index finger equals the internal state of feeling put down or scolded?"
4. As the experiencer presents this statement to each member, in turn let each member *meta-model* it by presenting an alternative meaning (a reframe). For example, "How would you like it (how would you feel) if you thought about the pointing finger meaning that the other has an unconscious 'schoolmarm anchor'?"
5. Play around with alternative meanings until the experiencer finds one that he or she finds resourceful and useful.

Meta-modeling Complex Equivalence (Part II)
1. In groups of 3 or 4 persons.
2. Begin by inviting the first experiencer to present some complex equivalence that doesn't serve them well in life (a negative association or anchor that evokes an unresourceful state). For example, "When I think about someone talking to me and pointing at me with their index finger, I feel put down or scolded."
3. Group members should first confirm the complex equivalence. For example, "So, for you, a pointing index finger equals the internal state of feeling put down or scolded?"
4. Once confirmed, as a team invite the experiencer to teach the group *how to do this constructive skill*. "If I took your place for a day so that you get a day off from this—how would I do this? What pictures, sounds, words, etc. would I use—their quality, nature, order, etc. so that I could 'run my brain' in this way?"

5. Deconstruct the *strategy* of the complex equivalence—until everybody feels satisfied that they have all the necessary ingredients for it. Then, taking turns, offer shifts and alterations in the strategy that will disrupt it. For example, "So when you see the pointing index finger with a blob of chocolate on the end of it ..."

Meta-modeling Empowering States
1. In groups of 3 or 4 persons.
2. Invite the first experiencer to describe a resource and/or resourceful state that he or she would like to have or to have much more (e. g. confidence, poise, self-affirmation, enthusiasm, love, energy, etc.). Once specified—invite the experiencer to describe this fully.
3. As the person offers their map of the resource—meta-model him or her in such a way as to invite a richer and fuller map of the experience until the person has fully stepped into that resource.
4. Let one of the group members kinesthetically *anchor* this resourceful state and ask for *an auditory digital term* that summarizes it—"Confidence, joy, calmness, etc." Anchor kinesthetically repeatedly—saying the term at the peak of the experience—until just the word anchors it.

Running The Operational Levels On The Meta-model
1. In groups of 3 or 4 persons.
2. Take the following list of statements—and read out loud to your group and brainstorm an exploration about the Meta-model violations that you find in it. *Quickly* list them.
3. Then identify the highest level Meta-model distinction that would provide the most useful information in making a transformational change in the owner of such a statement.

Statements: You always talk as though you're mad.
                It's impossible for me to trust people.
                My brother thinks our parents were abusive.
                Everybody knows that you can't change a
                bureaucracy.
                Communication is really hard for me.
                Running away doesn't help.
                I laughed at the irritating man.
                Why do you always bring up such stupid
                examples?
                Self-righteous people just burn me up.
                The overwhelming price of food disturbs me.

Distinguishing Cause-Effect And Complex Equivalences
    1. In groups of 3 or 4 persons.
    2. Work through the following list together as a group—
       determining which of the following statements you'd
       classify as a C-E or as a Ceq.

Statements: I know he loves me when he touches me.
                It makes me angry when my husband looks at me
                like that.
                If you really loved me, you'd call when you're
                going to be late.
                I know you understand me when you talk to me.
                You don't appreciate me anymore. You don't kiss
                me when you leave for work.
                Turning in your reports on time will le me know
                that you're truly a responsible person.
                My partner's pessimistic attitude has caused our
                recent financial slump.
                I want to stay here longer, but I know you'll get
                angry at me if I do.
                My depression came upon me because my
                husband constantly criticized my body.
                Your nagging has given me another headache.

Visiting The Land Of Nominalizations
1. In groups of 3 or 4 persons.
2. As a group, identify the nominalizations (processes turned into a noun) that you find in the following statements.

Statements: People always push me around.
Nobody pays any attention to anything I say.
I like friendly dogs.
I heard my mother-in-law yesterday gossiping about the neighbors.
One should always respect the feelings of others.
It's painful for us to see her like this, you know.
Let's not get bogged down in details.
There's a certain feeling in the room.
Everybody feels that way sometimes.

Finding Behavioral Complex Equivalences
1. In groups of 3 or 4 persons.
2. As a group decide on two or three Complex Equivalences that you want to play with as you seek to find the *behavioral equivalents*. This will enable you to practice eliciting and feeding back distinctions around the Meta-model distinction of Complex Equivalences. For example: love, trust, respect, confidence, ferociousness, etc.
3. The group then works with the first experiencer by asking, "How do you know when you *trust* someone? What does *trusting* mean for you in terms of see-hear-feel terms? How do you recognize *trust*?"
4. As the first experiencer presents his or her *behavioral equivalents* of trust, another member of the group adopts and runs this behavior. He or she should feed it back to A until A feels satisfied with the behavioral equivalents—that "Yes, that looks like, sounds, and feels like *trust*."

Fuzzification And Meta-Modeling Battling
1. In groups of 3 or 4 persons.
2. As a group, create the most convoluted set of sentences that contains *all* of the Meta-model violations. Robert McCrory prepared the following one, published in *Anchor Point* many years ago:

"People[1] are always[2] surprised[3] by learning[4] their efforts[9] equal the best[5] that others[6] believe must[7] be achieved[8] by experimentation[9], [10]."

   [1] Lack of Referential Index: Which people?
   [2] Universal Quantifier: Always?
   [3] Deletion: How specifically are they surprised?
   [4] Cause-Effect: How specifically does learning surprise people?
   [5] Comparative Deletion (best as compared to what?
   [6] Mind-reading: How do you know what others believe?
   [7] Modal Operator of Necessity: What if achieved by another method?
   [8] Unspecified verb: How specifically achieved?
   [9] Nominalization: experimentation achieves?
   [10] Lost Performative: Entire sentence—according to whom?

3. Once you have a list of 5 to 10 really good convoluted super-fluffy statements—Groups enter into the Battle of the Meta-Modelers, presenting a line and recording the amount of time it takes for the second team to identify all of the violations. After so many rounds (e. g. 5 each), the team with the lowest "time" wins.

Chart 2:2

The Meta-Model Of Language

Patterns/ Distinctions	Responses/ Challenges	Predictions/ Results
1. Simple Deletions		
"They don't listen to me."	Who specifically doesn't listen to you?	Recover the Deletion
"People push me around."	Who specifically pushes you	Recover the Ref. Index
2. Comparative And Superlative Deletions (Unspecified Relations)		
"She's a better person."	Better than whom? Better at what? Compared to whom, what? Given what criteria?	Recover the deleted standard, criteria, or belief
3. Unspecified Referential Indices (Unspecified Nouns And Verbs)		
"I am uncomfortable."	Uncomfortable in what way? Uncomfortable when?	Recover specific qualities of the verb
"They don't listen to me."	Who specifically doesn't listen to you?	Recover the nouns of
"He said that she was mean."	Who specifically said that? Whom did he say that you call mean? What did he mean by 'mean'?	the persons involved Recover the individual meaning of the term
"People push me around."	Who specifically pushes you?	Add details to the map
"I felt really manipulated."	Manipulated in what way and how?	
4. Unspecified Processes—Adverbs Modifying Verbs		
"Surprisingly, my father lied about his drinking."	How did you feel surprised about that? What surprised you about that?	Recovers the process of the person's emotional state
"She slowly started to cry."	What indicated to you that her starting to cry occurred in a slow manner?	Enriches with details the person's referent
5. Unspecified Processes—Adjectives Modifying Nouns		
"I don't like unclear people." "The unhappy letter surprised me."	Unclear about what and in what way? How, and in what way, did you feel unhappy about the letter?	Recovers the speaker's projected sense of feeling "unclear" or "unhappy."
6. Universal Quantifiers		
"She never listens to me."	Never? She has never so much as listened to you even a little bit?	Recovers details about the extent of a process and counter-examples.

7. Modal Operators
(Operational Modes of Being)

"I have to take care of her." "I can't tell him the truth."	What would happen if you did? What wouldn't happen if you didn't? "You have to or else what?"	Recovers details of the process, also causes, effects, and outcomes.

8. Lost Performatives
(Evaluative statement(s) with the speaker deleted or unowned)

"It's bad to be inconsistent."	Who evaluates it as bad? According to what standard? How do you determine this label used, of "badness?" etc.	Recovers the source of idea or belief—the map-maker, standards

9. Nominalizations
(Pseudo-Nouns that hide processes and actions)

"Let's improve our communication."	Whose communicating do you mean? How would you like to communicate?	Recovers the process and the characteristics left out
"What state did you wake up in this morning?"	How specifically did you feel, think, etc.? What behaviors, physiology, and internal representations make up this "state?"	Specifies the verb and actions

10. Mind-Reading
(Attributing knowledge of another's internal thoughts, feelings, motives)

"You don't like me..."	How do you know I don't like you? What evidence leads you to that how a person knows	Recovers the source of the information— specifies conclusion?

11. Cause-Effect
(Causational statements of relations between events, stimulus-response beliefs)

"You make me sad."	How does my behavior cause you to respond with sad feelings? Counter Example: Do you always feel sad when I do this? How specifically does this work?	Recovers understanding of how a person views causation, sources, and origins—specifies beliefs about how world works

12. Complex Equivalences

(Phenomena that differ which someone equates as the same)

"She's always yelling at me, she doesn't like me."	How do you equate her yelling as meaning she doesn't like you? Can you recall a time when you yelled at someone that you liked?	Recovers how the person equates or associates one thing with another. Ask for counter-examples to the meaning equation.
"He's a loser when it comes to business; he just lacks business sense."	How do you know to equate his lack of success in business with his lack of sense about it?	Could other factors play a role in this?

13. Presuppositions

(Silent Assumptions, Unspoken Paradigms).

"If my husband knew how much I suffered, he would not do that."	How do you suffer? In what way? About what? How do you know that your husband doesn't know this? Why do you assume that his intentions would shift if he knew? Does your husband always use your emotional state to determine his responses?	Recovers the person's assumptions, beliefs, and values the he or she just doesn't question. Specifies processes, nouns, verbs, etc. left out.

Chapter 3

Inside Magic's Structure

Developments In Understanding And Organizing
The Meta-Model

"A word is worth a thousand pictures."
(Robert Dilts, 1979)

Bandler and Grinder did not initially present the model in a sequential or orderly way. When the first volume of *The Structure Of Magic* appeared it contained no list or chart of the Meta-model. In fact, you have to hunt and search to gather and synthesize in order to get the Meta-model itself from the book. In doing so, one will find some information about nominalizations in Chapter 2 and some more in Chapter 3. One NLP trainer described his experience this way:

> *"Those early NLP works just about drove me crazy. As I reflect back over the hundreds of hours I spent listening to, and transcribing tapes, and dissecting those gosh awful so-called books, it almost makes me ill. My students have no idea what I went through in order to present them that material in an understandable and sequential form."*

Further work followed what began to put the model into an orderly form using charts and outlines. Dilts (1975) seems to have been the first to have identified 11 of the Meta-model distinctions in a paper, "Application of the Meta-model to the Socratic Method of Philosophical Inquiry" that he later published in 1983 as *Applications of Neuro-Linguistic Programming*.

During the late 1970s, 80s, and 90s, charts contained from eight to thirteen Meta-model distinctions. The largest number that I've heard of came from NLP Trainer, Charles Faulkner, who said that he had found 17 patterns. By contrast, only eight appeared in *Magic Demystified*, a 1979 book by Byron Lewis and Frank Pucelik. Although, they did end up with twelve by putting five sub-patterns under "Referential Index" (pp. 76-83).

During the intervening years, numerous developers and authors suggested various structures for organizing, understanding, and working with the Meta-model. In this chapter, I will explore some of the ideas of the expanding Meta-model.

Formatting And Structuring The Meta-Model

The very first formatting of the Meta-model occurred in 1976 with the second volume of *The Structure of Magic*. There Bandler and Grinder suggested the following as "useful in organizing our experience both in therapy and in training seminars":

1. Gathering Information
2. Identifying the limits of the client's model
3. Specifying the techniques to be used for change (p. 165).

About the same time, Dilts (1975) suggested the following three categories as "the natural groupings of the Meta-model violations":

1. Information Gathering
    a. Deletions (Del)
    b. Unspecified Referential Index (URI)
    c. Unspecified Verbs (UV)
    d. Nominalizations (Nom.)
2. Setting and Identifying Limits
    a. Universal Quantifiers (UQ)
    b. Modal Operators (MO)
3. Semantic Ill-Formedness
    a. Complex Equivalence (CEq.)
    b. Presuppositions (Ps.)
    c. Cause-Effect (C-E)
    d. Mind-Reading (MR)
    e. Lost Performative (LP)

In this organizational form of the Meta-model, Robert emphasized the value of the Meta-model for (1) high quality information gathering, (2) setting and identifying personal limits in one's model of the world, and (3) working with, identifying, and expanding the quality of one's meanings in life. Dilts (1983a) wrote:

> *"For me, this is what the Meta Model is all about: being able to increase your efficiency in anything by finding out that kind of specific information. Knowing anchoring, knowing strategies, or any technique by itself isn't going to get you anywhere unless you know how and when to use them. ...The Meta Model is all about asking these kinds of questions. What do you need? What would happen if you did?"* (p. 5)

As an information gathering technology, the Meta-model grew from Richard's and John's noticing (and modeling) *the style and nature of the kind of questions* that the therapeutic wizards, Virginia Satir and Fritz Perls, asked. Such questioning explicates understanding about how a given *model of the world* works, what comprises its elements, the linguistic structure of it, and how a person "knows" what he or she knows. Thus the most basic and essential questions the Meta-model asks involve the very heart of epistemology:

What do you know?
How do you know?
How do you know that you know?

Organizing Magic Via Representational Systems

Another attempt at structuring and ordering the Meta-model occurred earlier. Lewis and Pucelik (1982) attempted to correlate the Meta-model distinctions to the representational systems of visual, auditory, kinesthetic, and auditory-digital. Thus, as they presented each distinction, they offered generalizations wherein they attempted a correlation.

> *"This [Reversed Referential Index] is a common pattern used by individuals operating from the kinesthetic system."* (p. 82).

> *"Remember that 'visuals' organize experiences in such a way as to prevent 'contact' with those around them."* (p. 83)

> *"This Meta-model violation, unspecified verbs, is particularly common to individuals operating out of the kinesthetic category."* (p. 91)

> *"This pattern [The Modal Operator of Necessity] is typical of someone operating out of the visual model, especially under stress. In this way, a 'visual' can verbally externalize his frustration or anger at a person or situation and at the same time exclude himself from having any responsibility for the situation."* (p. 95)

Though this certainly provides an interesting speculation between possible correlations in people's surface language expressions and underlying sensory system (the VAK), this set of correlations does not seem to fit for most people, and so we do not find it carried over into many other works.

A Linguistic Anchoring System

Part of the way words work involves how they elicit or "anchor" associations to sensory-based referents and memories of experiences. Thus, in part, *words operate as anchors of representations.* If we think of a strawberry, the White House, a zebra, your childhood home, or Donald Duck—what *comes to mind* involves the sensory based facets that we have associated with such terms. Therefore the Meta-model functions as an explanatory paradigm for **how** we put together our linguistic anchoring system as we attempt to "make meaning" of things.

Yet words not only "work" via their associative and representative nature, they also "work" via the process of eliciting frameworks of meaning, categories, contexts, and contexts of contexts. While Transformational Grammar began the current understanding of linguists about our internal transforms from a deep structure of representation to the surface structure expressions, later studies in Generative Semantics, Interpretative Grammar, and more recently Cognitive Grammar have shown that "meaning" also arises from the meta-level categories within the surface structures. These categories identify the *domains* or *contexts* that govern the meaning.

The Meta-model provides insights into both of these domains. It begins by working with the process of **how** we associate external sights, sounds, sensations, and experiences with internal structures (words, linguistic phrases, grammatical transforms, etc.). By using the modeling distinction of deletion, the Meta-model provides a way for us to discover the fuller range of these associations.

Yet it does more. The Meta-model also recognizes that we have construct, and use many higher level constructs (generalizations and distortions). Thus we create and use *class terms* of categories (hence domains of knowledge) as we move up into higher and higher levels of abstraction. There we "make meaning," not so much by mere word association and anchoring, as by the connotations, intentional definitions, categories, cognitive domains, and presuppositions at those higher levels. Here the Meta-model provides us a way to explore and identify our meanings, or neuro-semantics, at those levels and then to transform them so that they work in more enhancing ways.

Dilts (1979), in explaining the Meta-model, rephrased the old line about a picture evoking a thousand words to:

"A word is worth a thousand pictures."

Why? Because the *meaning* of any word, to any given person, *begins with* the pictures, sounds, and sensations that that word evokes within. It *begins there*. It does not end there. Meaning involves a lot more than mere representation.

Charles Faulkner, after studying extensively in the field of cognitive linguistics and grammar, noted that many NLP practitioners have narrowly assumed that the Meta-model only treats words in a rigid stimulus-response situation, "as conditioned responses."

(This comprises the "static words" of Korzybski that I will add to the Meta-model in Chapter four.) He asserts further that we should also recognize how that language itself operates in a semantically laden way—"human language is necessarily semiotic."

> *"You listen to somebody say they had an accident, or 'I am really troubled,' and you make sense of that for yourself without really knowing the other person's representations for it."* (Dilts, 1979, p. 12)

This partly occurs because *context* itself drives (or governs) representation. Thus we must explore the context domain—the person's encyclopedic knowledge of a domain and the context of that context.

Meta-Modeling Magic—
Present State To Desired State Algorithm

What then should we meta-model? Obviously, we do not need to meta-model everything. Rene Pfalzgraf (1989) noted this in an article on Meta-model III.

> *"Ineffective challenging usually occurs when the person challenging has no idea what they are going for; i. e. the NLP practitioner does not have a well-formed outcome. There are too many meta-model patterns present in each sentence to effectively challenge all of them."*

As an information gathering tool, if we meta-model every linguistic violation of ill-formedness—we will only overwhelm ourselves (and the other person) with too much information. A map does not have to detail *everything* in the territory. We can leave out trees, bushes, alleys, and all kinds of things on a city map and get around just fine. We can generalize the direction of a freeway without worry about putting in every angle shift. We can even distort the size of the freeway—coloring it red and making it very thick without deluding anybody that they will see the actual freeway as a mile wide.

How then do we make our decisions about what to meta-model? Dilts (1979) suggested an "algorithm" that later evolved into *the S. C. O. R. E. model*—namely, a person begins with *a desired state* from the position of *a present state*. From there, he or she will need various *resources* in order to operate as transitional mechanisms, thereby bridging from one state to the other. The S. C. O. R. E. model stands for:

> **S**ymptom— of the present state that we want to change
> **C**ause(s)— that contribute to bringing the symptom into existence
> **O**utcome— the desired state
> **R**esources— for moving from present state to desired state
> **E**ffects— the results that occur from the desired state

Continuing, Robert explained,

> *"One of the difficulties experienced by early meta modelers was gathering too much information. So, present state desired state is the overlay I want you to put on your information when you use the Meta-model. Essentially, everything else is going to be irrelevant other than present state and especially desired state information."* (Dilts, 1979, p. 33)

In the field of Brief Psychotherapy, de Shazer (1988) and associates refer to the same process in terms of **the miracle question**.

> *"Suppose that one night there is a miracle and while you are sleeping the problem that brought you into therapy is solved: How would you know? What would be different? How would your husband know without your saying a word to him about it?"* (p. 5)

We find a similar type of question in NLP. After we get a clear description of a present state, then we can ask about the desired state. Robert Dilts presented this in very much the same format as the miracle question—only he used the metaphor of **magic**.

> *"If you had a magic wand, what would you do differently? What would you see, hear, or feel?"* (Dilts, 1979, p. 33)

John Grinder did the same according to Robert (1979). Once upon a time John ran this pattern with a lady at a liquor store who had all the external signs of alcoholism. She needed a ride home, so he gave her a lift. As he did, she asked, "Why do you drink?" He answered the question in terms of liking the taste of wine and also said that he didn't drink very much. Then, "being the magician that he is," he asked her a meta-modeling question.

"But that isn't the real question you wanted to ask me, is it?"

She burst into tears. "No, the real question is 'Why do *I* drink? '" This evoked a lot more talk. Eventually, John shifted her from that present state to a desired state. He did so with a tease.

"But the question *why* do you drink is not really the question that you want to find the answer to either."

Then, after setting up more interest and tease, he said, "The real question is, 'What would you be doing if you weren't drinking?'"

This magical question shifts one from thinking about the problem state to attending to the nature and questions of *the solution state.*

Consider then what any question about "what would life be like the day after the miracle" evokes. It invites the respondent to begin to access specific sensory-based information about life apart from the problem. It also encourages one to associate into it and to personalize it. This begins to build, for that person, that new reality. No wonder, in terms of the Meta-model, **desired state questions** comprise some of the most important and life-changing questions.

> *What would it be like if you could experience X?*
> *What would you see, hear, or feel?*
> *How would you know that you experience X?*

Organized By The Modeling Processes

By the mid 1980s most charts organized the Meta-model in terms of the three modeling categories: Deletions, Generalizations, and Distortions. At first, they organized these lists from simplest to more complex (deletions to distortions). By 1987, however, many had turned this around, presenting the higher levels first as reflected in Figure 3:1 (this version from Tad James only had 10 distinctions).

In ordering the distinctions as indicating a logical level system, this draws attention to the fact that we have *deletions* in every distinction of the Meta-model. In Cause-Effect statements, we have deleted the connection. In Mind-Reading, we have deleted detailing the process of how we know or how we have made our guess about another person's mind, intentions, and motives. In Complex-Equivalence, we have deleted how we created the equation between the two items that exist on different logical levels. *Deletion*, as a modeling process that occurs in the other processes (generalization and distortion), thus represents a smaller unit.

Similarly, we have *Generalization* in most of the Meta-model distinctions. We generalize how things work in causing or leading from one thing to another (C-E). We generalize the basic pattern of meaning (CEq) as we specify what External Behavior (EB) equates to what Internal State (IS). We generalize about the basic thoughts, emotions, and intentions in others (MR). But conversely, we may have no generalization when we simply delete the specifics of who, how, when, where, etc.

Figure 3:1
Organization Of The Meta-Model

Distortions
- Mind Reading (MR)
- Lost Performative (LP)
- Cause-Effect (C-E)
- Complex Equivalence (CEq)
- Presuppositions (Ps)

Generalizations
- Universal Quantifiers (UQ)
- Modal Operators (MO)

Deletions
- Nominalizations (Nom)
- Unspecified Verbs (UV)
- Simple Deletions (Del)

By the time I wrote the notes for Richard Bandler in his Master Practitioner Training (1989) which later appeared in the book, *The Spirit Of NLP* (1996), Richard had made some other changes regarding the Meta-model.

For instance, first of all he **inverted** the Meta-model so that it began at the top with the largest level distinctions. He had moved "nominalizations" from the category of deletions to the larger grouping of distortions. Among the other changes, he had separated *presuppositions* from the category of distortions and had begun to use it as another modeling process. This also appears briefly in Lankton's (1980) work, *Practical Magic* (p. 54). There he noted it in two paragraphs, but did not develop the idea of the operational logical levels within the Meta-model.

Also, Richard Bandler and Eric Robbie presented this schematic of the Meta-model as a system of logical levels. Therefore, the higher modeling processes (presuppositions) *drive* (or organize) the levels below it, and the next highest process (distortion) drives generalizations and deletions below them (Figure 3:2), etc. More recently, I have noted this facet of the Meta-model as a system of logical levels in *NLP: Advanced Modeling Using Meta-States And Logical Levels* (1997).

Figure 3:2
Meta-Model In Logical Levels

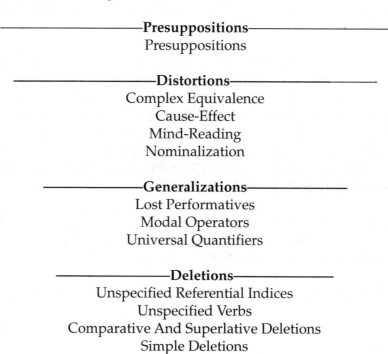

—————————————————**Presuppositions**————————————————
Presuppositions

—————————————————**Distortions**—————————————————
Complex Equivalence
Cause-Effect
Mind-Reading
Nominalization

—————————————————**Generalizations**—————————————
Lost Performatives
Modal Operators
Universal Quantifiers

—————————————————**Deletions**—————————————
Unspecified Referential Indices
Unspecified Verbs
Comparative And Superlative Deletions
Simple Deletions

The Magic At Operating At Higher Levels

What significance arises from re-structuring the Meta-model so that we recognize the logical level system inherent within it?

First, it highlights the fact that *higher levels organize and modulate the lower levels.* Thus Meta-model challenges and shifts at the higher levels will more pervasively effect, govern, control, and organize the changes and transformations at lower levels. This means that at the lowest level in the system (the *deletions),* we will get the smallest "chunk size" of information. Here indexing and asking for specifics will provide us single answer chunks of great precision. This gives us lots and lots of details that fill in the missing pieces, and yet these pieces may only address trivial concerns rather than crucial ones.

As we move up to *generalizations,* we begin to get larger chunks of information—beliefs, information about how a person has structured his or her world in terms of their *modus operandi* (MO), and their "rules" for living (LP).

When we get to the *distortions,* we have access to the person's internal world that deals with causation (C-E), meanings and associations (CEq), values and states (Nom), and beliefs about the states of others and what causes those states (MR). Yet the largest level of all flows from the person's presuppositions—those unspoken assumptions in their beliefs about knowledge, meaning, self, destiny, etc. (Ps.). Here we find a person's "undefined terms" (Korzybski).

Eric Robbie has suggested that, as we learn to think about the Meta-model involving such logical levels, we learn to ask ourselves logical level questions:

- What "chunk size" of information (from specific to global) do I need?
- At what level will I get the most useful and valuable information?
- At what level can I intervene to get the most pervasive impact?
- At what level does the person's difficulty exist?

The Magic Within Systems

Another valuable understanding arises from viewing the Meta-model in terms of a logical level system. As a *system* of interactions—we begin to recognize that what we do in one part of the system will have reverberations in other parts of the system. It alerts us to how "going meta" and moving up to higher levels will sometimes generate emergent **meta-level phenomena** that we can't explain as merely "the sum of the parts."

Thus from out of the mind-body system of representing data (non-verbally and linguistically), of working with symbols and systems of symbols, *emerges* new qualities and properties. This explains the power of beliefs (and beliefs about beliefs) in governing perception, body functions, autonomic nervous system operations, health, and experience. The Meta-States model more fully explicates this domain.

Even though our representations at any level may not accord with or fit the territory at all (and may represent nothing at all in the territory), as we represent it and then develop other thoughts-and-feelings (beliefs) *about* those representations, we thereby construct a system of thoughts-and-feelings about those. These higher level cause-effect relationships, complex equivalences, presuppositions, etc. will become **actualized** (literally, real-ized) in the body. The representations become somatized and so govern neurology.

When that happens—we truly have **neuro-semantic reality.** No wonder this generates "semantic reactions" (Korzybski)! From this, we begin responding to the world via our neuro-linguistic and neuro-semantic models of the world. As an attractor in a self-organizing system—it molds, governs, determines, and controls our "reality."

Prior to the Meta-model as an explanatory system, we would simply call this "magic." Now we know the structure of this magic. This opens our eyes about *how the "magic" works.* But we also know more.

We have access to knowing *the incantations of growth, potential, sanity, and resourcefulness.* Wherein does this lie? It lies in the same languaging processes of our nervous system-and-brain. So the same processes by which we create "black" magic which curses, defeats, sickens, toxifies, and destroys us—**the same languaging processes** also give us the power to create "white" magic by which we can bless, strength, and empower, make life whole and sound.

Grinder's Precision Model For Business

After Bandler and Grinder split up (about 1980-1), John Grinder teamed up with Michael McMaster to create a fascinating reduction/expansion version of the Meta-model. They designated this formatting, *The Precision Model* (1983/1993). They specifically designed this Meta-model adaptation for the context of business and management. They then offered it as a model and set of procedures for managers to obtain the highest quality of information possible. They sought to provide a "systematic way of controlling the quality of the language information" (p. 11) and to provide "information engineering skills" (p. 179).

In re-designing the Meta-model, they engineered the Precision Model it so that it would allow managers to accomplish several purposes.

1. Gather the highest quality of information.
2. Ask explicit questions to get precisely the information needed by directly responding to language cues— Pointers.
3. Determine the level of quality needed in a given context by using Frames and Frame Procedures.
4. Use various Frames for managing the process of moving from Present State to Desired State.
5. Learn numerous Procedures that maintain the frames to thereby guarantee efficiency.

Accordingly, they engineered *the Precision Model* with three sets of tools: Frames, Procedures, and Pointers. The *Pointers* reduce the Meta-model to five linguistic distinctions: unspecified nouns and verbs, modal operators, universal quantifiers, and comparative deletions. Thus we find in this Model a set of "tools to engineer information flow channels" (p. 30). They described the Meta-model distinctions (without ever labeling them as such) as **precision tools or technology** for converting low grade information into "high quality information necessary for precise planning and execution in business" (p. 45).

In *translating* the therapy-dominated language of the Meta-model for business contexts, they created a lot of new terminology. For instance, they labeled the Meta-model *distinctions* **pointers** and the effect of tracking from low grade quality to high grade quality as **blockbusting** (busting a block of over-generalized information). Thus:

1. First pointer—Noun Blockbuster (p. 54)
   (Unspecified Noun, Referential Index)
2. Second pointer—Verb Blockbuster (p. 57)
   (Unspecified Verb)
3. Third pointer—Universal Blockbuster (p. 62)
   (Universal Quantifiers)
4. Fourth pointer—The Comparatzor (p. 86)
   (Comparative Deletions)
5. Fifth pointer—Boundary Crossing (p. 176)
   (Modal Operators)

In this re-doing of the Meta-model, Grinder and McMaster called the *linguistic markers* **the special language markers.** Thus for a Comparator, they suggest *the Difference Procedure* by asking, "What is the difference between...?"

While this facet of the model *reduced* the full Meta-model, the next set of tools greatly expanded the Meta-model by bringing up meta-level phenomena that govern language—Frames or Contexts (anticipating the current developments in Cognitive Linguistics). Thus, the Precision Model delivers two kinds of tools

"a set of Frames which identifies and establishes the context or boundary conditions within which information is being elicited, and a set of Precision Model questions which develops the high quality information within that context." (p. 25)

Grinder and McMaster presented three basic Frames with five Procedures for maintaining the frames.

1. Outcome Frame: to identify and establish the target desired state, a verbal mapping of the outcome that the participants want to achieve. The outcome provides a context for focusing resources. It also provides an explicit standard of relevance and efficiency within which to organize information.

2. Backtrack Frame: a mechanism to review or trace the development of information maps relevant to the outcome. We can use it to verify a shared map or understandings and to establish a context for the next step. By backtracking, we are rephrasing in order to precisely summarize a development of understanding.

3. As If Frame: to establish a contrary-to-fact "context or frame in which the desired information or behavior then becomes available" (p. 134). Asking questions as if you didn't know the meaning of a term or phrase.

> "Let me pretend to be naive about this margins-inventory situation. Specifically, see how many ways you can describe to me that this problem might be solved."

Then, within these Frames—they offered six Procedures:

1. Evidence Question: "a powerful organizing device available to a skilled manager" enabling him or her to "get in a principled way contextualized to the point information" (p. 69). Present State/Desired State Frame—the most pervasive organizing principle in the model. "What will you accept as evidence?"

2. The Difference Question: "What is the difference between the present state and the desired state?" This specifies the steps and stages needed to move from one place to another. These stages involve: d*efining the difference, pathfinding, surveying, and evaluating.* Re-processing the Difference Procedure over and over focuses precisely the "problem" as "the difference" between present state and desired state.

Pathfinding describes the creative and brainstorming process of coming up with alternatives choices. The manager seeks primarily to tap into all of the available information in the individual maps and to co-create with the group a richer and fuller shared map. In pathfinding we move continually to more fully specified verbs until we achieve adequate precision.

Surveying refers to filling in the details of a path selected for reaching a certain outcome.

Evaluating finally makes a choice among the paths (alternatives) surveyed that will lead one to the desired outcome state. Here one makes a choice about a specific pathway.

3. The Efficiency Challenge: "What factors do you know that will eliminate this potential course of action?" This prevents wasting time on non-feasible alternatives.

4. Relevancy Frame: Designed to directionalize a discussion toward an outcome in a principled way by keeping the conversation on track and preventing "a veritable avalanche of free associations." A manager should challenge relevancy immediately and courteously.

> "Would you please connect that question with the outcome we're presently working on?" "I don't understand the relevance of that remark with respect to what we're doing here right now—please explain..." "... your last statement throws me—how is that pertinent to what this part of the meeting is about?"

5. Recycle Frame: looping back through a word or phrase that we find "so rich with potential hidden material" that we find it profitable to keep returning to enrich our map (p. 130). "How else might we .... [verb]?" "How else might we increase funds for investment?" "How else might we improve the quality of our product?"

6. The Missing Link Procedure: "How will that achieve what we want?" This specially adapts the Relevancy challenge in order to develop new branches of pathfinding.

By incorporating frames and procedures into their *Precision Model*, Grinder and McMaster essentially jumped up a logical level and expanded the Meta-model with some higher level linguistic phenomena. Cognitive semantics and grammar speak about this in terms of *domains, contexts,* and *categories.* Here we move up from *the content* of a conversation between persons where imprecision and vagueness occur (see Chart 3:3). As we do, we move up to various larger levels *frames-of-reference.* And as we do, we meta-state the content thoughts-and-feelings by bringing thoughts-and-feelings about *Outcome* (where we want to go and what we want to achieve) to bear on the content. They also meta-stated by bringing the other frames to bear on the content, namely, *Backtracking* (refreshing our representations of where we have been), and *As If* (pretending and imagining future possibilities).

Chart 3:3

```
                       _____As If Framing_____>
Meta-Levels
        <____Backtracking Frame _____

        _____Outcome Frame_____>

Primary Level:   Person #1   <words/ non-verbals>   Person #2
Content
```

The Outcome Frame sets a larger domain that allows us to *think strategically* with the Meta-model. It enables us to continually step out of the content frame to check where we stand with the person or persons with whom we communicate. Not knowing where we stand in such a process (whether in business, parenting, negotiating, etc.) makes it almost impossible to know how to maintain appropriate context. "Information is precise only if it is in context." (p. 145).

"The Precision Model demands that you know where you are in the process and provides the tools enabling you to know. Failure to clearly differentiate where you are, this is, to be constantly aware of the context, often results in inappropriate responses to comments or information." (p. 143)

"The Precision Model not only enables a manager to know where he is at any time in the process of problem solving, it insists that he knows where he is. Maintaining context and specificity will be accomplished only if a manager knows where he is in the process." (p. 163)

The Meta-Model: Reductionistic Only Or Generative As Well?

In the process of "meta-modeling" we obviously *chunk down*. We move *down* the scale of specificity-to-abstraction as we elicit more and more specifics using the challenging questions. Bandler and Grinder noted that the overall effect of this leads to *de-hypnotizing* because it reconnects a person back to the deeper structure of the experiences out of which the map arose.

Zink and Munshaw (1995) noted this reductionistic power of the Meta-model in an article entitled, *Collapsing Generalizations and the Other Half of NLP.* Their overall critique urged NLP practitioners not only to engage in reduction, but also to move up the scale of generalizing. Yet in offering their critique, they seemed to have drawn several unfounded conclusions about the Meta-model.

"That the Meta-model is a deductive tool should be extremely obvious, as its primary function is to reason from the general to the specific. It deconstructs generalizations; it roots out distortions and recovers deletions." (p. 20)

Because it reduces, Zink and Munshaw argued that NLP generally has developed too much of a reductionistic attitude and has developed too little use of induction in the sense of building up generalizations. They presented this as having contributed to fewer and fewer new developments in NLP during the 1990s.

> *"We think we know why there has not been more truly generative change in the field of NLP in recent years ... the major problem is: an over-reliance on reductionistic thinking and paradigms."*(p. 17)

> *"Many NLP procedures—the V-A-K Strategies Model, the Sensory Submodalities Model, and Meta Model of Language in particular—are intended to reduce Map scale."* (p. 24)

Now while the Meta-model certainly focuses, primarily, in chunking down, it also contains processes that encourage us to "chunk up." Bandler and Grinder illustrate this in the transcriptions entitled, "In the Vortex" (Chapter. 5). By "just" meta-modeling a client, they have the therapist saying,

> *"Let me get this straight: you're saying that your mother's not noticing what you did for her means that she wasn't interested in you?"* (p. 127)

They then commented, "The client again verifies the generalization involved." Thus **verifying generalizations** describes one important purpose (and process) of the Meta-model.

T: "Ralph, have you ever had the experience of someone's doing something for you and you didn't notice until after they pointed it out to you?"

T: "The therapist decides to challenge the client's generalization—here he chooses to begin the challenge by shifting the referential indices ... and therefore, the generalizations are transformed." (pp. 127-8)

Here we have two additional meta-modeling processes—**shifting referential indices** and **transforming generalizations.** When we shift references and apply a statement back to the speaker, it not only challenges the statement, but frequently invites the speaker to construct the generalization *as applied to him or her.* They may have used a map that they never applied to self. This response would therefore invite the speaker to create a new generalization. And sometimes this creates great insights as the person accesses counter-examples to their other generalization. The result? *A new,*

more balanced generalization.
T: "Did you not notice what they had done because you weren't interested in them?"

R: "No, I just didn't notice..." (p. 128)

Here the client *drew a new conclusion* (or generalization). He chunked up and in doing so this move accomplished two things. First, it began to deframe the old generalization and, second, it transformed it into a new one. In fact, in the meta-modeling that followed, the therapist shifted referential index time and again. Each time it had the effect of eliciting from the client *a new generalization*—one that would more effectively enhance his life.

The same occurred when the therapist challenged the Modal Operator. The client said that he didn't communicate his love directly. To this the therapist asked a meta-modeling question, "What prevents you from telling her?" In eventually answering that "nothing stopped him" and that he guessed he could, *he had to build a new generalization*—a new map that allowed him to so answer. This offers another means of evoking a person to "chunk up" to a new understanding using a Meta-model challenge.

"What stops you? ... The therapist uses the technique of asking for the generalization, the outcome of the client's actions which he finds scary." (p. 134)

Here Bandler and Grinder expressed meta-modeling as **asking for the generalization.** Interesting enough, it evoked this response that involves a logical level shift.

"Nothing, that's what so scary. (laughing)" (p. 134).

The first statement ("Nothing") reflects that he could not find or create a generalization that would now fit his model of the world. Here the client has a generalization. For this "nothing" signifies the existence of a "no-thing," or as we might say, a blank. As he *chunks up* to a higher level to consider "what stop him," he becomes aware that no-thing stops him. Then to that awareness, he immediately experiences another. "That's what so scary." He *chunks up* one more time as his consciousness **reflects back** onto its previous product ("nothing") and entertains some lighthearted scariness *about* it.

Undoubtedly some trainers and writers may have overlooked **the chunking up** facets in the Meta-model, and therefore emphasized only the reductionistic processes. Yet the Meta-model itself does not function *only* in that way. Certainly the challenges or questions of the Meta-model chunk down as it asks for more specifics, indexes time, place, person, context, etc. Yet the model itself, as it explains the three modeling processes also chunks up. It shows how we abstract from the deeper structures to create our maps.

Meta-modeling then involves summarizing and articulating the unarticulated generalization that the person simply uses as his or her presupposition. We see this demonstrated in "Transcript 2" (pp. 134-153). When the client said that she "kinda hinted" to her roommates to let them know what she wanted, the therapist asked, "How do you kinda hint?" She said, "I do things for them."

"Then, since you do things for them, they're supposed to know that you want them to do something in return?"

Comment: "The therapist decides to check to see whether the client will verify this generalization ... by repeating the entire generalization to the client." (p. 142).

Here, **articulating a presupposition,** as in fully expressing a person's generalization and then having him or her verify it, chunks a person up to the generalization—and then up above that to do "an ecology check" on it. In this case, it worked. First the client said "It sounds sorta funny when you say it like that." This indicates a meta-level awareness of an evaluation *about* the generalization. Specifically, the person continued to comment *about* the statement.

> *"Like I'm not being honest or something, but you just can't go around demanding things all the time or people will not want to give them to you."* (p. 143)

Moving to a meta-level, via this Meta-modeling type of questioning, evoked *an even larger level generalization.* In fact, shortly thereafter, the therapist discovered that this statement brought him to *the very edge of her map.*

T: "What prevents you?"

B: "I just can't, ... I JUST CAN'T."

T: "Beth, what would happen if you asked for something when you want it?"

B: "I can't because people will feel pushed around if I ask for things from them." (pp. 146-7).

Then *shifting referential index* again, "Are you aware that ... you came to me and asked if I would work with you?" (pages 148-9), "the therapist relativized the client's generalization." As soon as she recognized that, he then applied it back to her situation. And as he did, it enabled Beth to create a new and more enhancing generalization about herself and about speaking more assertively about her requests. All of this illustrates the inductive power and usage of the Meta-model.

The Type Of Thinking Inherent In The Meta-Model

In my opinion, Zink and Munshaw (1995) have generated another misunderstanding of the Meta-model. Defining a "generaliza-tion" as "the act or process of deriving or inducing a general conception, principle, or inference from particulars" (Oxford English Dictionary) they then concluded that the definition of generalization was wrong as given in **The Structure of Magic** (p. 216).

> "*A generalization is NOT 'the process by which a specific experi-ence comes to represent the entire category of which it is a member.'*" (1995: 21)

They explained their analysis as follows:

> "*That's an entirely different breed of cat and is more properly called categorization—reasoning by category. A generalization describes or defines the essence of a class, while categorization merely stands in for any member of a class. Categories remain concrete and literal while generalizations are figurative and symbolic because they are abstractions.*"

Lakoff (1987), an earlier proponent of Transformational Grammar who later developed Generative Semantics, and then went on to work in the field of Cognitive Linguistics, wrote a book on category distinctions. In it he enumerated *several kinds of categories,* although he primarily made the distinction between the classical theory of categories (Aristotelian) and prototype theory (from Eleanor Rosch). In his work, he analyzed the prototype theory of categories as involving several features including family resemblances, extendable boundaries, central and non-central members, goodness-of-fit, radical structures, idealized cognitive model, etc. In other words, we have many different kinds of "reasoning by category," and not just one monolithic kind of "categorization," especially the Aristotelian form of category alluded to by Nelson and Joe.

The same holds true also for "generalization." We can distinguish different kinds and qualities of generalizing—generalizing at different levels of concreteness and abstraction. Synthesizing and distilling a number of instances of something (e. g. work situations) will lead to a "generalization." Using the Aristotelian classic definition of category, Zink and Munshaw conclude:

> *"If the work Map contains the essence of multiple and varied work conditions then it is a generalization; should it be reducible to a single instance, it is a categorization."* (1995: 22)

However, to use Rosch's and Lakoff's prototype theory of categories, the first instance simply articulates the heart of the generalization, while the second offers an example of the generalization that has such "goodness-of-example" that it operates as a prototype. The multiordinality of the term "generalization" allows for this much flexibility in meaning (See Chapter. 4 for multiordinality). For me, this completely calls into question the following judgment:

> *"One of these principles, Surface/Deep Structure, holds that our Maps can be reduced to single concrete examples. If this is true, then the Surface/Deep Structure concept precludes abstract thought."* (1995: 22)

I do not buy this as the original intention in *The Structure of Magic* regarding the Meta-model nor in the original Chomskian model as Transformational Grammar. Asking "specifically what, when, who, where, etc." does not *necessarily* imply that "our Maps can be reduced to single concrete examples." It only implies that asking such sends a map-maker back to his or her internal references. Doing this sometimes deframes the maps because they cannot find specific concrete cases. At other times, it confirms the maps inasmuch as the person does find some prototypical instances. This enables the person to explore the degree their reference supports the generalization, the degree it does not, to look for characteristics left out, distortions, etc.

The Meta-Stating Power Of The Meta-Model

If the Meta-model and the meta-modeling questions/challenges not only "chunk down" but also "chunk up," then such questions can evoke and facilitate *meta-states.* This raises some important questions.

Do we see such in the original work of Bandler and Grinder?

Do we have any examples of *meta-stating* in *The Structure of Magic?*

Yes, I believe so. Already, we have looked at this exchange in that original work that illustrates how meta-modeling encourages a person to "go meta" and access a meta-level state of awareness.

> "T: 'What stops you?'
> R: 'Nothing, that's what's so scary.' (laughing)" (p. 134)

In addition, consider this quote that models the meta-level shifting that Richard and John found in Satir's work:

> "When you ask questions like, 'How do you feel about that?' (whatever that might be) you are, in fact, asking your client for a fuller representation (than even the Deep Structure) of your client's experience of the world. And what you are doing by asking this particular question is asking for what you know is a necessary component of the client's reference structure. ..."

Here, at the very beginning of the development of what they would later designate as "the NLP model," Bandler and Grinder address the two directions that consciousness can take. First of all, at the primary level, it moves *outward* to the world and then, second, it moves back and onto the experience and products of consciousness (i. e. the thoughts, emotions, etc. that we produce).

In the first case we experience our thoughts-and-emotions **going out** to the world beyond us—to the events, experiences, and words that we encounter there. Here consciousness engages the world and wraps itself around information, then represents it, processes it, and responds to it.

In the second case, we experience our thoughts-and-emotions **reflecting back onto itself.** We call this "self-reflexive conscious-ness." As we experience it, we move up a logical level since our thoughts-and-feelings no longer take access of that "out there"— but of things "inside." In the first, we experience thoughts-and-emotions **about** something external. In the second, we experience thoughts-and-emotions **about** something internal.

"How do you feel *about* your feelings *about* this experience?"

In the *Meta-States Model* (Hall, 1995), I defined a **meta-state** as simply *a state about another state,* hence a mind-body state that has reference to a previous mind-body state. This moves us to a meta-level when we experience meta-level phenomena: thoughts about thoughts, feelings about feelings, second-order abstractions (Korzybski), self-esteem (Bandler and Grinder), etc.

> *"This new question, which is characteristic of Satir's work, is: 'How do you feel about your feelings about what is happening? 'This is essentially a request on the part of the therapist for the client to say how he feels about his reference structure—his model of the world..."* (p. 160-1).

To illustrate, Bandler and Grinder provided an illustration of a client upset and angry because Paul "just doesn't care about cleaning up the house." Upon discovering that Paul directly and clearly stated this and that this represents no mind-reading, they ask:

"How do you feel about his telling you he doesn't care...?
I feel angry...
How do you feel about feeling angry?
How do I feel about feeling angry?
Yes, how do you feel about feeling angry at Paul?
Well, I don't feel so good about it." (1975: 162-3)

In explaining this, Bandler and Grinder noted:

"The therapist ... chooses to shift levels, asking the client about her feelings about her image of herself in her model of the world...The client appears to be initially confused by the therapist's question requiring her to shift levels. This is a common reaction to such level shifts in our experience..."

Here we have another meta-modeling process and questioning that obviously *"chunks up"* and moves a client to **higher levels.** It even shifts **logical levels** since the questions facilitate a person moving up the scale of abstraction and generalizing at a new level. What seemed to have prevented Bandler and Grinder at that point in their formulations from recognizing this as *a meta-stating process* involves the meaning language that Virginia Satir gave them. Satir said that any answer to the question, "How do you feel about feeling X?" results in articulating the person's "self-esteem."

"Changes at this level—the level of self-esteem—are extremely important, since a person's self-image affects the way a person organizes his entire experience or reference structure. Therefore, changes at this level of structure permeate the client's entire model of the world." (1975: 162-3)

"This question is extensively used by Virginia Satir in her dynamic therapy—she describes this question as an excellent way to tap the client's self-esteem (the client's feelings about his feelings)—a part of the client closely connected with his ability to cope..." (1976: 57)

As they accepted the assumption that this *reference structure* of a person's reality, a meta-level structure, which *"permeates the client's entire model of the world"* as a definition of "self-esteem"—they failed to see the extensiveness of this level. Today, in the Meta-States Model, we recognize the structure of "self-esteem" as only one of the many **meta-level phenomena** that we construct there. Multiple other meta-level phenomena and structures similarly result from consciousness reflecting back onto itself.

This means that we can use the meta-modeling challenges and questions not only for reducing and deframing impoverishing maps, we can also use them to chunk up to create new enriching generalizations. This occurs, in fact, regularly, whenever we ask:

> And what stops or prevents you?
> How do you feel about experiencing those thoughts or feelings?
> How would you like to think-and-feel about that?
> What does it mean to you when you think or feel about X?

Such meta-modeling elicits a person to reflect back on the products or experience of previous states—thereby evoking or creating a *meta-state experience*. It leads them to shift up to a higher logical level.

Conclusion

Since its introduction, numerous insights, additions, re-organizations, usages, and extensions have occurred with reference to the Meta-model over the years. The extensions of the model mentioned here have obviously enriched it, expanded it, and given us more ways to do *magic* in our minds-and-emotions-and-bodies.

But what about additional language distinctions to the original 13? What, additional extensions to the Meta-model distinctions themselves have arisen? Let's now turn to this subject.

Chapter 4

Adding More Magic

The Wizard Korzybski
And His Magic

[In this chapter I have taken all of the references
from Alfred Korzybski's (1933/ 1994) Science and Sanity.
Page numbers in parentheses such unless otherwise noted.]

The Meta-Model of language (Chapter 2) enables us to understand *how we can do "magical" things by languaging*. Our languaging creates our models of the world, which, in turn, govern how we perceive, feel, think, and act. The *distinctions* of the Meta-model alert us in recognizing and examining not only the content of our maps, but their *very form* and *structure*. With that ability we can examine the effect than such on our paradigms. Further, as our constructed realities (our maps) affects our bodies, neurology, emotions, behaviors, and skills (the magic we experience), alteration of the map inevitably transforms our experiences.

The practical value and usefulness of the Meta-model arises from how it begins by utilizing *our everyday expressions*. These "surface structure" statements provide us a pathway to the mapping processes that generated them. This gives us a linguistic path via the *Meta-model neuro-linguistic distinctions* for hearing and recognizing a person's "model of the world." Tuning our hearing to various *linguistic markers* we can actually detect or identify semantic ill-formedness.

So what?

Our ability to detect ill-formedness in a mental map—a poorly designed map, whether our own or another's—equips us with some *especially empowering understandings*. First, we get an immediate awareness of, and *feel for*, the map-territory distinction. Then, almost simultaneously, we recognize that the "problem" may arise partly, or even solely, as a poorly constructed map. This shifts our focus in terms of problem-solving and responding. A marvelous and highly useful consequence follows—we don't need to get mad at our map or someone else's map. After all, "It's just a map."

And if "just a map," then it doesn't exist as a form of some genetic pathology. The problems we experience arise primarily from *poor mapping*. This alerts us to the fact that we may have simply left out important data. Or it may alert us that we have created some abstract generalizations about things as classes or categories of concepts that may not accurately, or usefully, correspond with the territory. It may suggest that we have altered or transformed structures, relationships, meanings (semantics), associations, etc. in unenhancing ways. It may imply that we have started from assumptions that do not facilitate our navigating life well. Somehow we have simply not mapped out something in a way that promotes our well-being. But now we can!

We value by examining our maps in terms of **semantic well-formedness**—a well-constructed map. If *"the menu is not the meal,"* and we have a real abbreviated menu, we may simply want to expand the menu choices. If we have a really old menu, we may want to update it to make it more current. If the menu has become folded, smeared,or dirtied so we cannot even read it—we may want to completely replace it.

The Meta-model entirely avoids the entire epistemological questions about the "truth conditions" of the map. Rather than evaluating whether we have "true" or "false" maps, it focuses on more pragmatic concerns:

- *Will our maps guide us to the places we want to go?* (i. e. healthy relationships, success at work, ability to achieve important goals, personal health and vitality, bonding, conflict resolution, etc.)

- *Do our maps have a structure that basically accords with the territory?* (Korzybski said that "structure and structure only" comprises the essence of "knowledge.")

- *Do we have enough flexibility and openness in our maps to keep updating them as circumstances and events change?* (Rigid maps carved in stone will eventually become dated and un-useful. In a process universe, we need flexible maps that allow us to keep adding to knowledge and to take feedback into account.)

- *Will our maps allow us to navigate effectively in the territory that we want to move in?* (Thus we run an "ecology check" regarding our map's effectiveness to make sure that our maps offer an ecological balance to all of the sub-parts of the system. In doing this, we thereby add "effectiveness" as a criterion to "accuracy of structure.")

- *Do our maps allow us a reflexive look at the maps themselves?* (Do we even recognize our thoughts, emotions, values, beliefs, etc. as maps so that we can evaluate our maps, de-construct maps, and re-map as needed? To do so keeps our mapping processes as an open system rather than a closed one.)

Extending The Meta-Model

The 13 distinctions of the Meta-model (Chapter Two) offer linguistic distinctions about modeling, map-making, and well-formedness. Yet they do not express the last work about such. John and Richard noted this at the beginning of their work in *The Structure of Magic*,

> *"...our Meta-model covers only a portion of the verbal communication which is possible..."* (p. 107)

> *"... we suspect that some of the research currently being conducted in Generative Semantics ... will be particularly useful in expanding the Meta-model further."* (p. 109)

So what *additional distinctions* can we find, identify, and develop to *expand* the Meta-model of language? What other typical linguistic distinctions occur in our everyday expressions of thought and ideas that can also cue us to ill-formedness, deletions, generalizations, distortions, and presuppositions?

I began my own search for *missing Meta-model distinctions* in 1990 as I explored in depth the foundational work of neuro-linguistics in the classic work of Alfred Korzybski, **Science and Sanity: An Introduction to Non-Aristotelian Systems and General Semantics** (1933/1994). Thereafter, I published a series of articles in **Anchor Point** (the USA magazine) on these missing Meta-model distinctions (1992). These were later published in German (**Multimind—NLP Paktuell** magazine) and Russian. That work ultimately culminated in my doctoral studies and dissertation and a book, *Languaging* (1996), which reflects that original work. Here I have replicated some of that work, updated it, and expanded it.

Nine Missing Meta-Model Distinctions

Bandler and Grinder certainly built their neuro-linguistic model utilizing many of the ideas that they cultivated from Korzybski. Yet they did not seem to bring over many of his actual linguistic distinctions (his *extensional devices*) into NLP. Indeed, since they took most of their distinctions from Transformational Grammar, they seemed to have passed over many crucial distinctions that Korzybski wrote about—which not surprisingly fit more with the current developments in Cognitive Linguistics.

As the founder of General Semantics, Korzybski focused primarily on *neuro-linguistic distinctions* that help us avoid **confusing** map and territory. As an engineer, he applied his genius to building a new language system that would offer a structure more in accordance with the territory and with the human nervous system. As he studied mathematical systems, physics, biology, neurology, etc., he developed a vision of promoting the human sciences (he called it "human engineering") that he would base on **a new Non-Aristotelian system of language**—General Semantics.

This non-Aristotelian system highlights the "laws of thoughts" that Aristotle made explicit—upon which classical "reasoning," "logic" and "categorizing" depended. Korzybski vigorously disagreed with these so-called Aristotelian "laws of thought." Of Aristotle's three "Laws" that he proposed govern Reality and thought/linguistics, we have the following:

1. *The Law of Identity:*
> I n Reality:
>> "Whatever is, is."
>> "A thing is what it is."
> In Linguistics:
>> "A word means what it means."
>> "A term's meaning must remain constant in any discourse."

2. *The Law of Contradiction:*
> In Reality:
>> "A thing is not what it is not."
>> "Whatever does not exist is non-existent."
> In Linguistics:
>> "A word does not mean what it does not mean."
>> "Two negatives make an affirmative."

3. *The Law of Excluded Middle:*
> In Reality:
>> "A thing either exists or it does not exist."
>> "A thing cannot have contradictory properties."
> In Linguistics:
>> "A proposition is either true or false."
>> "Two contradictory propositions cannot both be true."
>> "A class is either included in another class, or it is not."

Korzybski built General Semantics to specifically offer a non-Aristotelian system of languaging and theorizing about reality. For Korzybski—we have the following:

1. *The Principle of Non-Identity*
We live in a process world comprised *not* of "things" or substance, but ultimately of energy manifestations and communication. So nothing ever remains the "same." External reality consists of "a dance of electronics" and internal reality of communication, messages, and differences. We can only say, "For the sake of discussion, let's assume A will remain constant."

2. *The Principle of Contradiction*

More accurately we can say, "We should not classify a thing as both A and not-A at the same time in the same context." Because the observer always operates as a performer in the reality—the observer inevitably affects the reality.

3. *The Principle of the Middles*

More accurately we reformulate this "law" as, "We may classify a thing as existing or not existing, at the time regarding the same context." We can evaluate a proposition as true and false given different levels of abstraction, contexts, times, observers, etc.

NLP represents another *non-Aristotelian system,* developed in part from Gregory Bateson and others using General Systems Theory, cybernetics, communication theory, and other disciplines. The Cognitive Revolution has similarly built its models on a non-Aristotelian basis. Rosch (1975, 1977) and Lakoff (1987), many current cognitive psychologists, and those in cognitive linguistics, have similarly moved away from the old Aristotelian model and "logics." The old classic theory of logic portrayed logic as disembodied (hence not *neuro*-linguistic), transcendental (and therefore unaffected by an observer and not involving a performer), and absolute (hence not relative or context-dependent).

Extending The Meta-Model

I have derived the first seven distinctions from Korzybski and General Semantics. These linguistic markers cue us about different forms of ill-formedness that hinder us doing good human design engineering in our neuro-linguistics. (As a point of historical note, Korzybski coined the phrase, "neuro-linguistics" in his 1936 "Neuro-semantic and Neuro-linguistic Mechanisms of Extensionalization" published in the **American Journal of Psychiatry**. He also coined "human engineering" in his 1921 book, **The Manhood of Humanity**. During the 1940s, he conducted general-semantic workshops that he called "Neuro-Linguistic Trainings.")

Urged on by these additions to the Meta-model, I have included two others distinctions which I think further extend our tool box of neuro-linguistic markers. At the end of the chapter I have used a graphic box designed by Dr. Bodenhamer to summarize the distinctions.

1. Over/Under Defined Terms (O/U)
2. Delusional Verbal Splits (DVS)
3. Either-Or Phrases (E-O)
4. Multiordinality (M)
5. Static or Signal Words (SW)
6. Pseudo-Words (PW)
7. Identification (Id.)
8. Personalizing (Per.)
9. Metaphors (Mp)

In so extending the Meta-model with these distinctions for better map-making, I have reformulated seven Korzybskian distinctions using the format that fits with the Meta-model. I have packaged them in terms of neuro-linguistic **"distinctions"** and **"challenges"** to poor map construction (ill-formedness). Doing this allows us to make these distinctions explicit in a way that Korzybski did not in any of his original formulations. This further allows us to combine and synthesize these new and additional patterns into the Meta-model which thereby updates and expands the Meta-model. This gives us more secrets for performing neuro-semantic magic.

"Meta-model distinctions" here refer to those *language patterns* that indicate a structural form of languaging. These distinctions appear as "surface statements" (Chomsky, 1965) as we language ourselves and others using words and symbols. Yet these forms often create conceptual limitations that thereby impoverish our world.

To address this impoverishment, we "challenge" or question the linguistic structure. By so **meta-modeling**, we invite a person to re-connect to *the experience* out of which the map arose and to re-map it more fully, appropriately, and usefully. We do this specifically by offering a question, response, or challenge that elicits from the person more specificity in indexing the referents or the construction of a more enhancing map. This meta-modeling process thereby engages the person's mapping processes and thereby activates unconscious processes (the "deep structure," Transformational Grammar or the over-arching hierarchies of "cognitive domains" and "matrixes of domains" (Cognitive Grammar). This initiates the magic of change.

1. Over/Under Defined Terms (O/U)

Bandler and Grinder mentioned Korzybski and the role of "extensional" and "intensional" definitions in *The Structure of Magic, Vol. I* (p. 56), although they misspelled these terms. Korzybski described these two orientations and labeled them *over/under defined terms*.

He said that we mainly **over-define terms** when we operate out of an *intensional orientation*. This means moving into the world by assuming that our dictionary definition of terms offers a complete and satisfactory form of mapping.

> "We live, happy or unhappy, by what actually amounts to a definition, and not by the empirical, individual facts less coloured by semantic factors. When Smith$_1$ marries Smith$_2$, they most do by a kind of definition. They have certain notions as to what 'man', 'woman', and 'marriage' 'are' by definition. They actually go through the performances and find that the Smith$_1$ and his wife, Smith$_2$, have unexpected likes, dislikes, and particularities—in general, characteristics and semantic reactions not included in their definition of the terms..." (p. 415)

Korzybski asserted that we have **over/under defined** most of our terms. We over-define (or over-limit) words **by intension** when we over-trust our formal verbal or dictionary definition. As we over-believe in our definition of the word as "real," we give it too much substance and concreteness. We under-define words by using too little **extension** (failing to use sufficient specific facts and details). This results in our generalizations becoming merely hypothetical (p. lii).

How does this relate to making a sane adjustment in the world (physical and psychological health, effectiveness in business, career, relationships, parenting, etc.)? Korzybski noted that when we primarily orient ourselves in the world by intension, this creates maladjustment. We then perceive, think, and evaluate reality by over-definitions, confusing our maps or "verbalisms" with the territory. We fail to evaluate by extensional facts when we do not operationalize our terms. Doing so would assist us in creating a better adjustment. This explains why *the deletion challenges* in the Meta-model work so "magically" to enrich our lives. As we become more specific, we index our concepts to specific people, times, places, and contexts. This interrupts the habit of over-generalizing which often shows up as "terriblizing," "awfulizing," "negative predictions of the future," "personal-izing," etc., as noted by Albert Ellis in Rational-Emotive Therapy (1976).

Consider what happens when a woman finds and marries "a good husband." This conceptual linguistic reality ("a good husband") exists, totally and absolutely, **not** as something in the world, but as *a verbal definition in her mind*. To the extent that she fails to recognize this, she sets herself up for disappointment and neurological shock, and will suffer some semantic reactions. She will find the meal very different from what she thought the menu offered!

The same occurs with all other generalized terms that exist only in the mind. We over-trust evaluative terms (in contradistinction to sensory-based words) like beauty, ugly, good, bad, productive, useful, wonderful, exciting, traumatic, etc. In this, our intensional orientation itself can do us harm—significant harm.

To orient ourselves exclusively in the world by means of inten-sional definitions of words dooms us to *a hallucinatory adaptive style*. This style treats *words* as if "real" and their formal dictionary definitions as "real." This does not promote sanity or adjustment. It will not do us good if we want to do valid reality testing or to effectively adjust ourselves to reality. S. I. Hayakawa (1980) described the difference between **extensional and intensional meanings.**

> *"The extensional meaning of an utterance is that which it points to or denotes in the extensional world... the extensional meaning is something that cannot be expressed in words, because it is that which words stand for. An easy way to remember this is to put your hand over your mouth and point whenever you are asked to give an extensional meaning.... The intensional meaning of a word or expression, on the other hand, is that which is suggested (connoted) inside one's head. Roughly speaking, whenever we express the meaning of words by uttering more words, we are giving intensional meaning, or connotations. To remember this, put your hand over your eyes and let the words spin around in your head."* (pp. 61-62)

Utterances may have both extensional and intensional meanings. "Angels watch over my bed at night" certainly has several intensional meanings, but no extensional meanings.

> *"When we say that the statement has no extensional meaning, we are merely saying that we cannot see, touch, photograph, or in any scientific manner detect the presence of angels."* (p. 62)

This Intensional/Extensional distinction provides a very valuable discrimination. Because **extensional statements** partake of an empirical and sensory-based nature, we can use them to bring an argument to a close. "This room measures fifteen feet long." No matter how many guesses we make about the room from our intensional definitions, all discussion ceases when someone produces a tape measure.

Not so with **intensional meanings**. Here discussions and arguments can go on world without end. "You have decorated this room in a really *nice* way." This statement can provoke all kinds of disagreements, because the speaker has not based it on "sense," but based upon "non-sense" evaluations, meanings, and definitions. The utterance does not refer to sense data at all; so one cannot collect sense data to settle the discussion. The speaker's statement does not refer primarily to the external world—but to his or her *internal world of evaluations*.

To question these linguistic forms of poor map-construction (ill-formedness), do the following:

a. **Chunk down** the over-defined words of intensional statements. This will evoke a richer representation of the person's meanings and references. Ask the person for extensional evidence of their intentional meanings. Ask the person to *operationalize* his or her meaning in see-hear-feel language (e. g. behavioral terms).

b. **Explore a person's presuppositions** in their undefined terms. Ask, *What does this assume? What have you presupposed in stating this?* This gets them to put their epistemology out on the table.

c. **Train this extensional orientation into your nervous system.** Korzybski noted that this represents the natural order of evaluation (i. e. facts first, then evaluations).

2. Delusional Verbal Splits (DVS)

This phrase highlights the General-Semantic emphasis on the danger and problem of *"Elementalism"* which refers to compartmentalizing and dichotomizing elements of a whole. Korzybski said that we often take reality-as-a-whole and, by conceptualizing and languaging, split it up into parts. Afterwards we forget the map-territory distinction so that we begin to treat the map "elements" as if real (e. g. having a separate existence).

We speak about "mind" and "body" as if we can have one without the other! We do the same with "space" and "time." Korzybski noted the revolution in physics that resulted when Einstein healed the delusional verbal split between "space" and "time." As Einstein re-languaged it (i.e. the "space-time" continuum), this holistic understanding led to the field of quantum mechanics. Korzybski suggested a similar healing for other forms of delusional splitting of the world: "mind-body," "thoughts-emotions," "neuro-linguistics," etc.

Using words, we can sort, separate, divide, and categorize the ever-connected flow of processes of the world. By words we can split up, sort out, organize, and punctuate the flux of reality. Doing this allows us to create theories, understandings, hypotheses, etc. Verbally also (but not actually), we can split up the world by the way we language our conceptualization. n fact, by languaging we inevitably **dichotomize** reality's rich interconnectedness. This creates "elements" or pieces. Later if we forget that we have so slaughtered the territory in our mapping, we begin to believe that the elements exist as separate entities. This Korzybski called "elementalism."

In languaging we can talk about "body" *and* "mind," "emotion" *and* "intellect," "space" *and* "time," etc. The referents of these individual words **do not exist in reality as separate elements**. They *cannot* so exist as separate elements. Their existence involves an interconnected process—a system of interactions. We can only split them *at the verbal level* in thinking and talking about the parts of things. In linguistic form (mental conceptual form) we treat them as separate words. This makes them "elementalistic" and to that extent false-to-fact—they do not accurately represent the territory.

Since we cannot actually or literally separate "emotions" and "intellect," this division structurally violates the organism-as-a-whole generalization (p. 65). So with "body" and "soul," and other **verbal splittings.** By them we typically confuse understanding, hamper development, and create false-to-fact ideas. In a word, we construct a very poor and inadequate map that misdirects and impoverishes. An elementalistic terminology assumes a sharp division between "mind" and "senses," "percept" and "concept," etc. Korzybski (1933/1994) wrote,

> *"Einstein realized that the empirical structure of 'space' and 'time' with which the physicist and the average man deal is such that it cannot be empirically divided, and that we actually deal with a blend which we have split only elementalistically and verbally into these fictitious entities."* (p. 106)

> *"The elementalistic 'absolute' division of the 'observer' and the 'observed' was false to facts, because every observation in this field disturbs the observed."* (p. 107)

If we create or use such *verbal splits* and fail to remain conscious that our words exist *only as words* (verbal representations), and only deal with verbal representational reality, we train ourselves in delusional semantic reactions. We train ourselves to think in terms of one-valued or two-valued semantics rather than recognizing the infinite valued world (pp. 194-5).

> *"In life, as well as in science, we deal with different happenings, objects, and larger or smaller bits of materials. We have a habit of speaking about them in terms of 'matter'. Through a semantic disturbance, called identification, we fancy that such a thing as 'matter' has separate physical existence. It would probably be a shock to be invited seriously to give a piece of 'matter' (give and not burst into speech). ... I have had the most amusing experiences in this field. Most people, scientists included, hand over a pencil or something of this sort. But did they actually give 'matter'? What they gave is not to be symbolized simply 'matter'.*
>
> *The object, 'pencil', which they handed, requires linguistically 'space'; otherwise, there would be no pencil but a mathematical point, a fiction. It also requires verbally 'time'; otherwise, there would be no pencil but a 'flash'."* (pp. 224-5)

To challenge a delusional verbal split and the elmentalisms within it, do any of the following.

a. **Hyphenate** the Verbal Delusional Split. When you catch elementalizing and dichotomizing in language, stick in *hyphens*. Korzybski said this functional process enables us to reconnect holistic processes that we can only separate verbally. "A little dash here and there may be of serious semantic importance when we deal with symbolism" (p. 289). Hence, "time-space," "mind-body," etc. Organism-as-a-whole words provide representations that remind us of the systemic nature of the world. It reminds us of the holistic and inseparable processes with which we deal.

b. **Question the elementalism.** *Does X (the DVS) truly stand alone? What context does X occur within? Can we deal with X without also considering Y or Z?*

c. **Create holistic terms.** For instance, use psychosomatic, semantic reactions, neurophysiology, psychobiology, attitude, a mental-emotional state, etc.

d. **Look for the systemic processes—the interconnected domains.** Develop an "eye" and awareness for systems of interactions. This will help to overcome the Aristotelian elementalistic perspective and equip us with *systemic thinking*.

3. Either-Or Terms and Phrases (E-O)

Another Aristotelian way of thinking involves viewing and languaging things in either-or terms, thereby creating two-valued terms. Yet with most things in the world, this maps another false-to-fact distinction inasmuch as it leaves out the excluded middles, continua, both-and perspectives, and degrees. It creates over-simplifications and two-valued dichotomies.

When we make statements phrased in Either-Or formats, we represent the territory and orient ourselves to that representation, as if we only have two choices in viewing, valuing, and responding. Typically, this causes us to polarize back and forth between the only two choices. Yet this seldom accurately represents reality.

We have created an Either-Or orientation and set of representations in psychology with the classic heredity/environment, nature/nurture, genetic/learning debate. Yet such false-to-fact concepts assume that we can divide an organism's characteristics into two distinct classes: one due to heredity, the other to environment. The excluded middle of Aristotelian logic drives this kind of thinking. "A thing either exists or it does not exist." This formulation excludes any kind of interaction as a third possibility. Yet human experience obviously involves *an interaction* of genes and environment, inherent hard-wire nature and the nurture we receive along the way.

Either-Or thinking does provide broad outlines regarding things at the gross level: day or night, cold or hot, water or land, etc. But when we exclude any middles—we create a very limiting map. A thing may stand as "true" or "false" in terms of our evaluations. And it may also stand as "ambiguous," "meaningless," "doesn't apply," or the indeterminate, "I don't know" category.

Either-or statements, structurally, assume a two-valued cause-effect thinking (pp. 216-7). Frequently this offers an over-generalization resulting from the failure to take into account levels of abstraction and the nature of multiordinal and infinite-valued terms.

To challenge these:

a. **Reality test the Either-Or structure.** Does this truly reflect an either-or situation? Can I discover any choices in-between, any grays, or other considerations which may enter into consideration and influence my representation of this reality? If I think about the two poles presented by these terms, what lies on the continuum between them?

b. **Explore the possibility of Both-And.** Could we have overlooked that in some way, at a larger frame, or in different contexts, both of these seemingly opposite responses stand as true? In what way could we consider both of these choices as accurate and useful?

Classes And Kinds Of Nominalizations

In the current field of linguistics, scholars have begun to specify many different kinds of nominalizations. This certainly makes a lot of sense. After all, we can make many distinctions in the kinds, qualities, and properties of *processes and actions*. For instance, we can distinguish actions that involve completed and incompleted processes, those that involve primarily one person, two persons, or more. We can distinguish processes of external actions and internal "mental" states, those of the past, the present, the future. Langacker (1991) distinguishes bounded and unbounded regions of actions.

Accordingly, in the following Korzybski distinctions, we have nominalizations that have taken on additional usages and qualities.

4. Multiordinality (MO)

Some nominalizations take on such a quality that they essentially lose any specific meaning and become so broad and general that we can use them at many different levels of abstraction. At that stage of development, these forms stand for no specific referent. They only have an over-generalized meaning, and the meaning changes according to *the level of abstraction* or context. Korzybski termed these infinite-valued terms **multiordinal**. These terms also have *a reflexivity* so that we can use them on themselves. Linguists describe such terms as *polysemy* or *polysemous*.

Multiordinal words involve a deletion of *the level* or dimension of abstraction and a generalization. We can then use them on many different levels of abstraction. These multiordinal, infinite-valued terms include many of the most common terms we use. We also argue about these highly *ambiguous* terms and seldom take the time to identify the level of abstraction that we have reference to.

> *"Mankind, science, mathematics, man, education, ethics, politics, religion, sanity, insanity, iron, wood, apple, object, etc. We use them not as one-valued terms for constants of some sort, but as terms with inherently infinite-valued or variable referents."* (pp. 138-9, 433)

A majority of our terms consist of names for *infinite-valued stages of processes with a changing content*. This makes them multiordinal in nature. As infinite-valued variables they are not true or false, but **ambiguous** in meaning. Consider "love" as multiordinal. We use the term to describe our thoughts and feelings about people and things (objects on the primary level), but we also use it in reference to concepts. "I love democracy." These exist as non-objects inasmuch as we construct them. We can even go further, "I love my love of democracy."

To challenge multiordinal nominalizations, do any of the following:

a. **Use co-ordinates.** Use co-ordinates to assign single values to the variable (p. 139). Identify **time** co-ordinates or **space** co-ordinates to contextualize the specific referent. If a word or phrase expresses ambiguity, to understand its meaning we have to contextualize the level or dimension of our use. This makes the multiordinal word specific.

b. **Supply a context.** Since these words essentially operate as terms without a context, supply a context for them in order to determine usage and meaning. By supplying a context we fix its meaning and make it single (p. 436).

c. **Chunk down** to the specific referents at each level of abstraction. Develop "a behavioristic and functional set of words" to map with specific descriptions. Using descriptive language orders the happenings on the objective level in sensory-based terms (p. 264). Doing this operationalizes our terms. Functional words enable us to translate dynamic processes into static forms and static processes into dynamic forms. Korzybski wrote,

> *"In science, we have to use an actional, 'behavioristic', 'functional', 'operational' language, in which we do not say that this and this 'is' so and so, but where we describe extensionally what happens in a certain order. We describe how something behaves, what something does, what we do in our research work..."* (p. 639)

d. **Check for reflexivity.** The test for multiordinality involves checking to see if we can reflexively turn the word back onto itself. Distinguishing multiordinal words as those that can operate on many levels of abstraction enables us to recognize their nature and how they function in our languaging. Can you move to another level and still use the term?

"Do you love someone? Do you love loving them? Do you love loving love?" "Do you have a prejudice? What about a prejudice against prejudice?" "What science relates to this?" "Do you also have a science of this science?" This reflexivity test will not work with non-multiordinal words. "What a beautiful tree!" "Suppose you had a tree of that tree?"

5. Static or Signal Words (SW)

When we fix the context of a polysemous *multiordinal* term, we specify its meaning. This generates a specific and definite meaning. Yet if we do this in such a way that we construct a fixed and rigid meaning—then we construct a poorly built map—a *Static Word*.

Here we take a process, nominalize it into a polysemous, vague, ambiguous word—and then inappropriately lock it down by giving it a fixed, rigid, "true for all time," and absolute definition. Thus when a multiordinal term becomes static—we freeze it using Aristotelian logic (i. e., "Whatever is, is."). Later we use such terms, forgetting and confusing the map-territory distinction. We lock in a multiordinal word at one level to freeze it so that it becomes 'static' in meaning for all time. This gives it a one-valued significance, hence, a Static or Signal Word.

Our tendency to *nominalize* verbs (or reify processes) in the first place undoubtedly contributes to creating static, definite, and absolutistic one-valued statements (p. 140). Creating these static expressions induces us into absolutist and dogmatic states. We begin making statements that sound like pronouncements from heaven. Korzybski said that this creates a "legislative semantic mood," absolutisms, and "the deity mode." "We humans ... have a tendency to make static, definite, and absolutistic one-valued statements." (p. 140). Of course, this fits with the absolutism of the Aristotelian laws of logic quoted earlier. "Whatever is, is." "Nothing can both be and not be." "Everything must either be or not be."

Yet when we ascribe to nominalizations a quality and certitude they do not (and cannot) have, we emotionally load them with the result that they become "heavy terms." This inevitably has a powerful affect on our neurology. We then experience the words as *the things*. "The thinghood of words" results from the delusions we create by these static words. We then use our nervous systems as animals use theirs (as mere signals), instead as symbols. We come to believe without question that the words *"are"* the things they stand for. This shows up in the "is" of identify verbs.

Use the following means to challenge and question these linguistic maps.

a. **Loose up the Multiordinal term** made so rigid and absolute by indexing who used it at a certain level on a certain date in a certain way.

b. **Extensionalize.** Enumerate the collection of items out of which we create the generalization. Extensionalize by dating and timing the referents. *"Point out to me specifically what you mean."* Korzybski noted that *the extensional attitude* represents the only one that accords with the survival order and nervous structure (p. 173).

c. **De-infinitize the state** to make it semantically harmless. We do this by identifying the stages and variables within the static over-generalized word. We do this by indexing time and place and person. This communicates, "not true for all time, all space, all people, etc."

d. **Ask meaning questions.** *What do you mean by...?* As we understand that we use words to construct or evoke meanings, this enables us to recognize words as creatures of our definitions. They "exist" in an entirely arbitrary and optional way. At the verbal level, all words and sentences exist only as *forms of representations* that evoke semantic reactions in our nervous system.

The events outside of our skin exist as un-speakable, absolute, and individual. Our *words* about things *"are" not* those things. Words and things exist on different logical levels. Our words merely express a verbalization *about* things.

Static words convey a false-to-fact understanding which leads us to over-evaluate words and to treat them as "things." This falsely ascribes an objectivity to words that they do not, and cannot, bear. We avoid objectifying words when we ask, *What do you mean by that word?* This also provides us psychological "distance" from language so that we begin to *feel* it at the kinesthetic level as truly **not** the territory—but just our *map of the territory.*

As we make a move to a higher level, and ask the meaning question at that level, it prevents the semantic blockage that arises when we treat words statically. *What do you mean by that word? How does your use of this word contrast with X?*

6. Pseudo-Words Non-Referencing Words (PW)

When we push a multiordinal polysemous nominalization so far up the levels of abstracting and detach it from the extensionalizing feedback to reality—we ultimately create a non-referencing *Pseudo-Word.* This means that just because we can make a verbal *noise* or *spell out marks* on paper which look like or sound like words, this does not necessarily make them true words. Korzybski designated such pseudo-words as *"noises"* (in the auditory channel) and as *"spell-marks"* (in the visual channel).

Yet here we have linguistic maps that reference nothing. Nothing exists in the actual world or in the world of logic (logical existence) to which such words can stand as true symbols. These airy nothings—these verbal fictions—have no reality in any dimension. Yet if we use them to navigate through the territory and take action based on such—we can often fall into disasters.

When we use words that actually refer to nothing outside ourselves, we merely make noises. What shall we say of maps that allude to no actual territory? We might find them interesting, even entertaining. Science fiction depends on such. But shall we find them useful to conveying accurate information or orienting ourselves to reality? No. They only exist in the world of "mind" as *pseudo-words* which makes them very tricky. Why? Because they look like words, they sound like words, yet they do not reference anything real—whether in the world of physics or the world of meaning and communication. These **non-referencing words** have no referent. These **noises** made with the mouth or **marks spelled** on paper only give that impression.

How do we tell the difference between *true and pseudo words*? What criteria can we use? By definition, for a sound or image to function as a true word it must *operate as a symbol that stands for* something. It has an extensional connection with the world. To the extent that it stands for, or refers to, something, **it serves as a true symbol,** elicits internal representations, and mentally "anchors" the referent. If it does not, it *merely stands as a noise*. It refers to nothing. Before a noise or image can function as a symbol, something must "exist" (actually or logically). If it does not, then it simply functions as *a semantic noise*, hence a meaningless sign (p. 79).

Before a noise or a spell-mark can exist as a symbol, **something must exist**. When it does, the symbol can symbolize that existing thing, process, or concept. In language and "knowledge" we have two kinds of existences: *physical existence and logical existence.*

Thus *unicorns* do not exist in the external world of unaided nature. They do not belong to zoology. When we apply the word unicorn to the field of zoology, we employ a pseudo-word. If, however, we employ the word with reference to mythology or human fancy, the word there has a referent and so functions meaningfully as a symbol (pp. 81-82).

The ability to distinguish between words which operate as *true symbols* by symbolizing something that exists and those which function merely as *noises* represents a vital skill for clear communication, thinking, and reasoning. If we *use noises* as if they were words, we create problems for ourselves.

> *"One of the obvious origins of human disagreement lies in the use of noises for words"* (p. 82)

Korzybski calls this a form of fraud since it literally involves "the use of *false representations*." Korzybski illustrated this with the word *"heat"* (p. 107). He noted that grammatically we classify "heat" as a substantive noun, (actually a nominalization). Yet physicists labored for centuries looking for some "substance" which would correspond to the substantive "heat." They never found it. It does not exist. Today we know that no such *thing* as "heat" exists. So what exists? Manifestations of "energy" (processes) and interactions between processes that create or release thermo-dynamic energy. So we use a verb or adverb (thermo-dynamic) to more accurately represents the referent. We talk about **the process** of "thermo-dynamics" as two objects or processes interact.

Sometimes we use "heat" to refer to our *sense of temperature*, the result of thermo-dynamic energy. "Heat" speaks about a relationship between phenomena in motion. To use this non-referencing term as a word engages in *a linguistic fiction* false-to-facts. No wonder the scientists looking for "heat" found themselves ill-adjusted to reality. Here, the verbal symbolism of language did not point to anything; it had no reference. Linguistically, the word deceptively mapped a road that took people down a blind alley. Korzybski illustrated also with the word *"space"* (p. 228). "Space," in the sense of absolute emptiness, does not exist. As a word it stand as neither true nor false, but non-sense (a delusional verbal split). It makes a noise, yet it says nothing about the external world. It stands as a label for a semantic disturbance, for verbal objectification, for a pathological state inside our skin, for a fancy, not a symbol.

He illustrated non-referencing words also with the word *"infinity"* (p. 205). The term "infinite" refers to **a process which does not end or stop**. We use it legitimately as an adjective describing the characteristics of a process. Accordingly, we misuse it when we use it as a noun. So with the verbal fiction of "owning" or "ownership."

> *"We see the utter folly of racing to accumulate symbols, worthless in themselves, while destroying the 'mental' and 'moral' values which are behind the symbols. For it is useless to 'own' a semantically unbalanced world..."* (p. 549)

We label these verbal forms which have no actual referents as *pseudo-words*. These noises and spell-marks arises as mere mechanisms of our symbolism. They have the appearance of words, but we should not consider them words since they say nothing in a given context (pp. 137-8). In practical life, we often do not even suspect collections of noises or spell-marks in books to exist as non-referencing (p. 142).

Rational-Emotive Behavior Therapy (REBT) has highlighted common pseudo-words of unsanity that torment lots of people and send them to a pit of emotional hell. These include: "awful," "horrible," "terrible," etc. These words refer to nothing. They function only as *emotional amplification words* that exaggerate a situation which a person does not desire. REBT challenges this philosophical nonsense by having the client explain **why** they evaluate the world as "awful" or "terrible" rather than just undesirable, and what they mean other than intense dislike and aversion. "Why is this experience 'awful,' 'terrible,' or a 'catastrophe? 'I know that you don't like it and that you wish you didn't have to deal with it. I can see how unpleasant and distressful it feels, but why is it 'awful? '"

Realizing that many words have no referent enables us to **not** immediately "buy into" words. Many find this absolutely shocking, having so long confused map with territory. Yet once we make this distinction, we can develop a new automatic response to words. Namely, we first test words to make sure they serve as true symbols.

Ultimately, our thinking-emoting arises from our linguistics. We can think no better than we use language. If we use an antiquated, primitive, and false-to-facts language, we will think in primitive and inaccurate ways. If we language unsanely, using words without true referents, we will begin to think-feel unsane.

Francis Bacon, in the early seventeenth century, criticized "the idols of the market-place" and so addressed the issue of pseudo-words.

> *"The idols imposed by words on the understanding are of two kinds. They are either names of things which do not exist (... names which result from fantastic suppositions and to which nothing in reality corresponds), or they are names of things which exist, but yet confused and ill-defined, and hastily and irregularly derived from realities. Of the former kind are Fortune, the Prime Mover, Planetary Orbits, Elements of Fire, and like fictions which owe their origin to false and idle theories."* (Bacon, 1620, p. 68)

To challenge non-referencing words:

a. **Reality test** the reference. Challenge pseudo-words by *referencing* them. Date and time index the referents. *Suppose I could see-hear-feel this, what would I see or hear or feel? To what kind or dimension of reality does this word refer? In what domain?* Find out to what field the term applies.
b. **Explore** the possibility of the word as a non-referencing word. Could this word, term or phrase have no actual referent, but exist only as a fictional and constructed understanding? Does this linguistic symbol reference anything that has actual or logical existence?

7. Identity / Identification (Id.)
For Korzybski, *identification* represented the primary factor of unsanity in human functioning (p. lxxviii). He made that declaration because it represents the heart of Aristotelian logic (reasoning and thinking) and *the* basic structure that stands false to fact.

By **identity** Korzybski meant *identifying* phenomena on different levels or identifying a thing in an absolute way even with itself so as to not recognize differences. He said identity meant *"absolute sameness in all respects."*

Obviously, "all" in this definition makes identity impossible. If we eliminate the "all" from the definition, then the word *"absolute"* also loses its meaning. We simply have "sameness in *some* respects," an acceptable concept. We then understand "same" as "similar." The concept of similarity, in fact, would enable us to create, work with, and use generalizations, labels, categories, etc. appropriately. If we alter the ideas of "absolute" and "all," we no longer have "identity" at all, only similarity.

Korzybski further asserted that *identification* leads to many false evaluations and to the majority of evaluations that create unsanity. Identity as "absolute sameness in all aspects" *simply never occurs in the world or even in our heads* (194). Nor can it. Identification results when we fail to make distinctions. It reflects our confusing of differences between things, events, and orders of abstractions.

In the world we only deal with unique individual persons, events, and things. There only exists *non-identity* in the world of processes. Every event stands as unique, individual, absolute, and unrepeatable. No individual or event can exist as the 'same' from one moment to the next.

Identification begins early in life. Infants develop semantic reactions as they identify (or confuse, we might say "anchor") "things" existing on different levels. When the infant discovers that his **cry** brings food, then neuro-semantically, his cry **"is"** food (p. 201). His pre-word noises become intimately linked with the referent. In this way, we all learn to equate words with referents so that we feel "the map **is** the territory!" The child doesn't make that distinction, indeed a child *cannot* make such a distinction at that stage. Later, our "semantic reactions" to words and ideas arise because, at the neuro-semantic level, our nervous system fails to distinguish word and referent. If someone calls us "stupid," we have to fight to fend off that attribution. If we identify, we program our neurology to *experience* it as "real." We salivate in a stimulus-response way.

Identification erroneously evaluates the products of our thinking-and-feeling as having objective existence. Ascribing such external objectivity to words maps out untrue and unuseful representations. Evaluation only occurs in mind. It exists and operates only as a mental phenomenon at the level of thoughts [Wilber calls this *intellibilia* (the "eye" of intelligence) and not *sensibilia* (the "eye" of the flesh or senses, 1983, p. 67). He picked up this language and these distinctions from Immanuel Kant.]

Higher level *identifications* using multiordinal nominalizations can also occur. We take a neuro-linguistic "state" term (love, joy, fear, anger, disgust, etc.) and *identify* with it or any other attribution—and we can create high level forms of unsanity and even insanity. This Korzybskian language distinction thus grows out of a nominalization and also closely corresponds to a complex equivalence.

An *Identification* statement makes an equation between things on different levels of abstraction. Here we create an equation that involves a confusion of the multiordinal nominalization, "self."

"I am ... X."
"He is a X."
"She's nothing more than a X!"

These involve the two most dangerous forms of mapping false-to-fact (doesn't fit the territory at all), namely, **the 'is' of identification,"** and "the 'is' of predication."

The Is of Identification involves equating or identifying one's self with words, labels, definitions, understandings, etc. Humans in all cultures typically do this. We take our powers of functioning (thinking, feeling, speaking, behaving, relating, achieving, etc.) and identify with such. We identify with our beliefs, values, skills, roles, experiences, etc.

The Is of Predication involves predicating or asserting qualities. Neurologically, we even do this at the perceptual level. Hence, "The rose is red." Yet this actually fails to map *the interaction* of what we receive from the world and the contributions of our sense receptors (rods and cones). Predicating judgments (our evaluations, meanings) takes this to a higher level ("He is a jerk") as we *project* out onto the world our idiosyncratic evaluations.

These "ises" shows how one of the central linguistic makers of identification shows up in the **"to be" verbs** (is, am, are, was, were, be, being, been, etc.). David Bourland, Jr. (1991) has called the "to be" verbs—"the deity mode" of thinking and speaking."This is that!" "That's how it is!" The damaging "ises" thus take two primary forms: (1) *the "is" of identity* ("I am..." "You are..." "That is...") and (2) *the "is" of predication* ("The apple is red"). Bourland created **E-Prime** (English primed of the "to be" verbs) to eliminate this (see Appendix B: There Is No "Is").

Not all "ises" create unsanity. When we use *"is" as an auxiliary verb* ("Jim is coming over," "Sally was going shopping") this "is" simply contributes and supports another verb. So it creates nosemantic difficulties. Nor does *the "is" of existence* do any harm. It simply points to events and things that "stand out" in our perception ("She is over there by the tree.").

Korzybski noted that the identification process inherently arises from the very form of our **subject-predicate language form** (pp. 198, 250, 57, 188-191). Our language patterns assume the existence of identification inasmuch as we form our basic statements we *speak of predicating* **things**. This presupposes an underlying level of existence comprised of *substances.*

When we engage in *identifying,* we experience a comparatively inflexible, rigid form of adaptation,low degree conditionality, and neurological necessity. Korzybski said that this represents an animal type of adaptation, and one most "inadequate for modern man" (p. 195).

Korzybski also noted that identification occurs in all known forms of "mental" illness. Yet in the world of process and non-identity (since every event exists as unique, individual, absolute, unrepeatable) no individual, 'object', event, etc., can exist as *the 'same'* from one moment to the next. So when we identify, **we create a mental illusion**—a fixed and rigid map. Thus by identifying, we begin to live in a delusional world of our own making.

> *"In heavy cases of dementia praecox we find the most highly developed 'identification'. [This] suggests that any identification, no matter how slight, represents a dementia praecox factor in our semantic reactions. The rest is only a question of degrees of this maladjustment."* (p. 568)

In identifying, we erroneously conclude that what occurs inside our skin (i. e. ideas, understandings, concepts) has *objective* existence. Psychologically, this leads to **projection.** We identify and then ascribe external objectivity to our words, ideas, meanings, etc. This generates a number of mental mapping mistakes: delusions, illusions, hallucinations (pp. 456-7).

To challenge identifications, to de-identify and to recognize the unique distinctions of reality:

a. **Extensionalize** to make specific what otherwise might become falsely identified. Korzybski said that *the extensional method deals structurally with the many definite individuals that distinguish and separate* (p. 135). We can extensionalize by indexing specifics (who, when, where, how, which, etc.), by making distinctions, by hyphenating, and by E-Priming our language.

b. **Differentiate** realities. Since "identity" never occurs in the world, by rejecting the very concept of the "is" of identity, we learn to orient ourselves more to differences and differentiation as fundamental (p. 93-4). This enables us to begin to look for, and specify, the absolute individuality of events. *How do these things that seem similar, and which you have identified, actually differ?*

c. **Sub-script** words with time-dates or space-locations (the indexing process). Such subscripting assists us in dealing with the absolute individuality of every event at every time. Since the world and ourselves consist of processes, every $Smith_{1950}$ exists as quite a different person from $Smith_{1995}$ (p. 263). This individualizing assists us in making distinctions. $Depression_{1991}$ differs from $depression_{1994}$; $depression_{Bob}$ differs from $depression_{Susan}$. By time-indexing we specify the date of our verbal statements. We can do the same with person-indexing, place-indexing, and even process-indexing.

d. **Practice silence at the unspeakable levels.** Training in recognizing "the unspeakable level of experience" describes a central technique for eliminating the "is" of identify. In the place of repressing or suppressing,

"we teach silence on the objective level in general... Any bursting into speech is not repressed; a gesture of the hand to ...the objects, or action, or happenings, or feelings. Such a procedure has a most potent semantic effect. It gives a semantic jar; but this jar is not repression, but the realization of a most fundamental, natural, structural fact of evaluation" (p. 481)

Notice how closely this technique corresponds to the early NLP technique of accessing the"stopping the world" state (McClendon, 1991, Grinder, 1987). This refers to stopping the world of one's internal dialogue. To do so moves us from the meta-level of language representations and brings us back down to the wondrous sensory rich world prior to our languaging of our "shared reality." It thereby facilitates us in creating a new mapping or languaging of our experiences.

Korzybskian Challenges

In this brief summary from the massive 760 pages of *Science and Sanity*, I have used the General Semantics terms, ideas, and *extensional devices* to extend the Meta-model. These empower us to challenge the structure of a linguistic map. Because some of these offer some new additions to our repertoire for responding to poor map construction (ill-formedness in syntactical and semantical constructions), I want to highlight them.

Hyphens. The device of hyphenating elementalistic terms enables us to stop the dichotomizing that splits up reality into parts and elements which results in inaccurate maps (e. g. organism-as-a-whole in a space-time world). This enables us to create more holistic maps that cue us to the interactive *systems* around us.

Indexing and subscripting. To index a word to a particular time, place, person, event, etc. by using a subscript gives the term much more specificity. As we so extensionalize, we create more clarity of thought and expression. Hence, $Science_{Aristotle, 300 BC}$ differs radically from $Science_{Einstein, 1903}$. In modern science we talk about this as *operationalizing our terms*. What specific behaviors, actions, responses, etc. would we see, hear, and feel?

Etc. The use of the term "etc." in General Semantics not only signifies "and so on," but also, "let the reader recognize and consider all of the other things that we could say and that we have not uttered the last word about this." Korzybski, in fact, developed a very extensive system for using "etc." in *Science and*

Sanity. He believed that the liberal use of "etc." would help to establish an *extensional attitude and orientation*. He believed it would promote a healthy tentativeness.

Silence. If our map only seeks to represent the territory and never "is" the territory, then learning to "stop the world" in terms of the chatty internal dialogue that runs in our heads or even the rush of our neurological VAK language (our sights, sounds, and sensations) gives us some deep structure awareness of the great gulf between the territory and all of our maps of it. In Korzybski's neuro-linguistic training, he would have people point at an object and maintain silence ... to anchor this awareness. "Silence on the objective levels" installs a strategy of psychophysical delay so that we don't react without thinking.

Quotes. Since words are not the territory to which they refer, cuing ourselves by putting especially slippery words in quotes alerts us to the danger of forgetting their map-like quality.

Another Wave Of The Wand—For Even More Magic

In addition to the seven linguistic distinctions from Korzybski, I have added two more that cue us about semantic ill-formedness in our map-making: Personalizing and Metaphoring.

8. Personalizing

From the field of Cognitive Therapy and REBT, Beck (1976) and Ellis (1979) have created lists of **cognitive distortions** that govern how we filter information and perceive the world. It may surprise some readers to know that most of these correspond very closely to the Meta-model distinctions.

[*Over-generalizing* corresponds closely to Universal Quantifiers and Lost Performatives.

All-or-nothing thinking corresponds to Universal Quantifiers as well.

Labeling fits with Nominalizations, Lost Performatives, Complex Equivalences.

Blaming goes with Lost Performatives—the judgments that we announce without identifying the map-maker.

Mind-reading precisely fits the Meta-model distinction by the same name.

Prophesying the future relates to what Bandler and Grinder termed "crystal-ball mind-reading" (1975, pp. 144, 147).

Awfulizing exemplifies a Nominalization and Lost Performative.

Should-ing obviously relates to the distinction of Modal Operators of necessity.

Filtering fits with all of the deletion patterns: Unspecified Referential Indices, Deletions.

Can't-ing relates to the Modal Operators of impossibility.]

Yet two distinctions from the list of Cognitive Distortions from these cognitive therapies do not seem to correspond to any of the Meta-model distinctions. These make up the categories of **"personalizing" and "emotionalizing."**

- **Emotionalizing** refers to using one's *emotions* for gathering and processing information. It thereby over-values "emotions" and treats one's emotions as an information gathering mechanism rather than a reflection of one's values in comparison to how one perceives things. In emotionalizing, a person reacts to things subjectively.

- **Personalizing** refers to perceiving things, especially the actions of others, as specifically targeted toward oneself as an attack on one's person. It refers to perceiving the world through egocentric filters that whatever happens relates to, speaks about, and references oneself. This sorting style obviously leads to an over-sensitivity to one's environment—typically one's social environment.

These ways of viewing things arise originally, as does *identification*, from the way a child's mind works early in life—egocentrically viewing the world in terms of self, assuming the world revolves around the self, and that most communication and events by others say something personal to us or about us. It works from the assumption that if I recognize something, I *have to* emotionally associate into it.

A person using these cognitive distortions sees, hears, and responds to information, events, words, etc. as if whatever occurs out there does so in a "personal" way—as a statement or reflection on the person.

In *personalization*, a person believes that he or she stands responsible for external situations for which they could not possibly stand responsible. "It's my fault that the picnic got rained out!" From that way of sorting things, the person then jumps to the conclusion that, if they so perceive things, they should *feel* such (emotionalize it). In "emotional reasoning," a person believes that *because* he or she feels a negative emotion, *there must exist* a corresponding negative external situation.

Such personalizing/emotionalizing shows up in language in the personal pronouns (I, me, mine), words indicating oneself, and in implied formats.

"Tom's making a lot of noise because he's angry *at me.*"

This expression involves a cause-effect ("because"), a complex equivalence (lots of noise equals= a state of anger), and personalization (the presupposition that Tom engages in the angry behavior and directs it at the person. Personalizing involves a higher structuring that attaches *personal significance* to events and communication that could just as easily be understood impersonally. It frequently lies behind (or above) other semantically ill-formed expressions.

Suppose someone says, "Linda is ignoring me." The way they have selectively focused on things (also discounting and negatively filtering) invites them to personalize. If we then can ask what that *means* to the person, he or she might say, "I will never have any friends." In this cause-effect statement, involving some universal quantifiers ("never," "any"), we also have another personalization, along with crystal-ball mind-reading of the universe!

"What does that mean?"
"It means I am all alone."

Personalizing not only feeds self-pity, but also "the entitlement syndrome," and when habitually over-used, the antisocial personality orientation. Joe typically ended work by catching a drink with the guys and then going home. As he entered his home, if he noticed that the children continued to play outside or watch TV when he arrived, his first automatic thought would be, "They don't care that I've been working hard all day." Similarly, if he arrived home late without calling and his wife Becky had already cleaned up the kitchen, he would automatically judge it. "That bitch never fixes a decent meal for me." If he then confronted her with that (!), and she didn't respond immediately with an apology, he would think, "She's ignoring me! How dare she!" This obviously sets the stage for more unhealthy interactions.

To challenge a personalization:

a. **Inquire the how.** *How* does the person know to treat it as personal rather than impersonal? "How do you know that Linda is intentionally ignoring you and doing it in order to send you a message?"

b. **Explore other possibilities.** "If Linda was just preoccupied, how would you tell? What would indicate that?"

c. **Go meta to explore the personalization** as a possible habitual meta-frame. "Do you typically read the behavior or words of others as saying something about yourself? Do you tend to be sensitive to yourself about such things?" "Could this represent a perceptual filter that you have learned to use?"

9. Metaphors/ Metaphoring
When we look at language at both the level of individual words and statements, we find **metaphors** everywhere. They *lurk in the corners*. They often *visit us* like *angels unawares*. At yet other times, we have to *smoke them out*. Most language, it seems, *operates* via the *structure* of metaphors. In fact, several theorists have

proposed that all language *boils down* to metaphor. Regardless, metaphor does seem to function as an essential part of how we conceptualize—we **compare** what we know with what we seek to know and understand.

Lakoff and Johnson (1980a) see metaphor as a basic process for structuring knowledge. They theorize that concrete conceptual structures form the basis for abstract thinking/talking.

> *"We understand experience metaphorically when we use a gestalt from one domain of experience to structure experience in another domain."* (p. 230)

Consequently, in thinking, perceiving, understanding, and talking we constantly find, create, and use metaphors from one experience to "make sense" of another. The fundamental nature of **metaphor** "is understanding and experiencing one kind of thing in terms of another." When we so use metaphors, we engage in a top-down kind of processing (deductive reasoning).

Analogical communication includes metaphors, analogies, similes, stories, and a great many other kinds of figurative language forms. Such language connotates and indirectly implies rather than directly denotes a referent. Such language endows communication with less directness, more complexity and vagueness, and more emotional evocativeness. It describes the language of the poet more than the scientist. I say "more," because scientists also use metaphor constantly, but more as an explanatory device, whereas the poet glories in it as an end within itself—for its beauty and charm.

To become sensitive to the metaphorical level and use of language, we need to think in terms of analogies and analogous relations. What term, terms, sentences, and even paragraphs imply or suggest some metaphorical relation? What metaphors does the speaker use to structure his or her thinking and framing? Lisnek (1996) has noted the "story" nature of communication and the Meta-model as a technology for addressing such.

"There is a term that applies to the story-telling model of communication—it's the 'meta' model. In simple terms, the meta model is based on the idea that people relate information in story form. As listeners of the story, we add to the information we hear or delete facts or impressions based on past experience and our interpretation of events. So, your version will assuredly be different from mine, even if we've both experienced the same event."
(pp. 33-34)

"When Arnie tells his best friend Mary about his rotten salary, he tells a story. ... The meta model of communication includes a set of patterns that allows us to examine how we generalize, distort, specify, or delete data as we relate information in our stories. We do this so that we can better position ourselves in negotiation by testing the stories of the other negotiator." (p. 34)

What metaphors occur in the following? "What you claim is indefensible." "She attacked the weakest point in his line of arguments." "His criticisms were right on target." "They shot down all my arguments." Since the overall frame-of-reference involves conflict, battle, war, we can identify such as the driving metaphors here. The speakers analogously compare the communication exchange to soldiers battling to win a war. How great this differs from another possible metaphor. "Arguing with him is like a dance." "We danced around the core issue for a long time." "The movements of our meanings whirled around with no pattern at first."

Metaphors typically operate at the level of **presuppositions** and so we usually experience them at meta-levels. This makes their presence and workings mostly unconscious. So when someone says, "Now I feel like I'm getting somewhere," we may not even notice the "travel" metaphor of journeying, adventuring, etc. "That was over my head" suggests a "space" metaphor to ideas and understandings.

Summary

As *a semantic class of life,* we map our internal reality and model of the world by using language. We can do none other. So to keep sane and productive in using language, we need to develop *consciousness* that whatever we say about anything does **not** exist as "the same thing as" that thing.

We live simultaneously in two worlds. We live in the world of what we call "objective reality," *Plethora* (as Bateson termed it, 1979) and secondly, we live in the world of symbols, meaning, or "mind," *Creatura* (Bateson's term to designate the world of communication, organization, semantic structures, etc.). In languaging, we operate at the verbal level of reality (the map level). Holding this in awareness as we language ourselves and others saves us from semantic reactions that arise when we confuse map with territory (Korzybski termed this process "identification").

The first seven linguistic distinctions mentioned in this chapter spring from the genius of the Korzybskian model about language, language behavior, and the effect it has upon "mind," thinking, personality, interactions, and everyday effectiveness. The last two come, respectively, from the work of Ellis and Beck in cognitive therapy, and then from my own observations.

In future works on *the secrets of magic,* I anticipate specifying other distinctions. Denis Bridoux, a UK NLP Trainer, and myself have recently explored several potential categories. In a recent training, we played with the category of *the Imposed Performative.* Here a person uses the "you" pronoun as if speaking about another while actually speaking of him or herself, or of general human experience. Functionally, this use of "you" operates in most instances as a hypnotic induction. "It's just that when you feel rejected, you wonder about your own worthwhileness, don't you?" A question to challenge this usage includes, "Is that what *you* think?" "Are you speaking about yourself or me?"

Together these extend the Meta-model of language so that we have more *linguistic markers* that we can use to cue us about possible impoverishment of our mental maps.

Extended Meta-Model Exercises
(In all of the following exercises,
do so in groups of 3 or 4 persons
unless otherwise indicated.)

- **Identification Exposure Exercise: "Who Are You—Apart from Are."**
    1. Introduce yourselves to each other for 3 to 4 minutes—presenting the kind of information you typically present as you disclose yourself. The only constraint: *the others will not allow you to use any of the "is" verbs.*
    2. Observing persons should listen for any of the "to be" verbs:
        is, am, are, be, being, been, was, were, and contractions
    3. "Beep" the speaker each time he or she uses an "is" verb. Totally disallow *the "is" of identity* and the *"is" of predication*—while permitting the auxiliary "is" or the "is" of existence.
    4. Switch so each person gets a 4 minute presentation.

- **Identity Statements in Complex Equivalences**
    1. Experiencer present a complex equivalence statement about self that he or she has found limiting and unenhancing.
        Example: "I am a failure." "I'm just not a math student."
    2. Responders take turns offering meta-modeling challenges (Ceq., Id., C-E., etc.) to loosen up the belief statement.
    3. After each round—invite the experiencer to offer a new self-statement that more emboweringly provides a better map. Continue until the experiencer feels satisfied with the new mapping.

- **Finding the Multiordinal Words of Life**
    1. Each person take turns describing a very positive experience of learning, growth, insight, personal development.
    2. Listeners write down as many nominalizations as they can hear and identify.
    3. Afterwards—compare lists and run the tests for multiordinality:

        At what level or in what context does this term apply?
        Can we apply this term to itself?
    4. Share with each other the level of specificity or ambiguousness that you experienced with the term.

- **Static Word Identification—Recovering "Process"**
    1. Relate to the others a negative emotional experience that you have experienced at some time in your life—or that you could experience. Describe what it meant to you, how you felt, etc. Do so for 4 minutes.
    2. Listeners write down as many nominalizations as possible.
    3. Debrief by comparing lists and running the tests for multiordinality

        At what level or in what context does this term apply?
        Can we apply this term to itself?
    4. Explore together which multiordinal word may have been turned into a **static word (sw)** thereby stopping the process world and creating a frozen universe of pain. Offer responses for inviting the person to remap with more process in his or her model of the world.

- **The Unsanity Show Down**
    1. Brainstorm together to generate a list of 10 examples of the following patterns that create limitations and problems—
        a. Identity statements
        b. Either-Or statements
        c. Personalizing
        d. Metaphoring

2. Two groups of 3 join together so that Group A match off with Group B, etc. Spokesman for the first group present the statements to the second group—inviting the second group to (1) identify the Meta-model distinction and (2) to meta-model it with an appropriate response.

- **Value Elicitation Exercise**
    1. Each person make a list of responses to the following statement.

    I hold X valuable and significant in personal relationships.
    X: _____

    _____
    I hold X valuable and significant in work and career.
    X: _____

    _____
    I hold X valuable and significant in parenting.
    X: _____

    _____
    I hold X valuable and significant in communication.
    X: _____

    2. *With one experiencer in the group—explore and fully identify the **behavioral equivalences** of his or her values. Translate back down into extensional language—What specifically would you see, hear, feel, etc. that would convey to you this X?*
    3. Pace the person's values back to him or her as you communicate the following message:
        As you learn these Meta-model distinctions and responses and practice them over the next few weeks and months—it will give you more X in your personal relationships, career, parenting, etc.

Figure 4:1

The Extended Meta-Model

Patterns / Distinctions	Responses/ Challenges	Predictions/ Results
1. Over/Under Defined Terms (O/U)		
"I married him because I thought he would make a good husband."	What behaviors and responses would make a "good" husband for you? do you use for the word "husband?"	Recover the extensional What references facts about the terms used.
2. Delusional Verbal Splits (DVS)		
"My mind has nothing to do with this depression."	How can you have "mind" apart from "body" or "body" apart from "mind?"	Recovers the split that someone has created verbally in language
3. Either-or Phrases(E-O)		
"If I don't make this relationship work, it proves my incompetence."	So you have no other alternative except total success or failure? You can't imagine any intermediate steps or stages?	Recovers the continuum deleted by the Either-Or structure
4. Multiordinality (M)		
"What do you think of your self?"	On what level of abstraction do you refer to "self?"	Recovers the level of "Self" can have many different abstraction that the meanings, depending on context and usage— speaker operates from. how do you mean it? Specifies the context and order.
5. Static Words (SW)		
"Science says that..."	What science specifically? Science according to whose model or theory? Science at what time?	Recovers the deleted details
6. Pseudo-words (PW)		
"And that makes him a failure."	What do you mean by "failure" as a word that modifies a person?	Challenges a map that uses words that have no real referent.
7. Identification (Id.)		
"He is a democrat." "She is a jerk."	How specifically does he identify with the term "democrat?" In what way? Upon what basis do you evaluate her using the term "jerk?"	Recovers the process of Identification or prediction. Invites one to create new generalizations.
8. Personalizing (Per.)		
"He does that just to irritate me."	How do you know his intentions? How do you know to take these actions in a personal way?	Challenges the process of personalizing.
9. Metaphors (Mp)		
"That reminds me of the time when Uncle John..."	How does this story relate to the point you want to make?	Recovers the isomorphic relationship between the story and the person's concepts.

Chapter 5

Magically Resourceful

Magic Formulas
For Making Life More Of A Party

We have now reviewed, summarized, and updated the Meta-model of language. Where does that bring us to? What "magic" does this meta-modeling allow us to perform? How can we use this model to perform "magic" on our own minds-and-emotions, and those of others?

In this chapter, I will present some of the neuro-linguistic and neuro-semantic **magic** that we derive from the NLP model.

"Hey! Where's The Magic?"

In the USA in the 1980s the Burger King hamburger chain rain a series of commercials wherein a "little ole lady" kept asking, *"Where's the beef?"* She didn't want some tiny little shriveled up burnt burger that could get lost in a bun. She wanted "the real thing." But when she peered under the gigantic bun, she didn't find the real thing.

A similar thing has often occurred in the fields of therapy, consultation, communication enrichment, empowerment of human resources, learning acceleration, etc. In the end, we frequently find the helpings under the bun very sparse. "Hey! Where's the beef?"

By application, we ask, "Where's the magic?"

In human neuro-linguistics, *the magic* occurs due to the interface between map and territory. As we construct images, schemas, paradigms, or models of the world and *use them to navigate* as we move through life—they become "magical" to us in that they form, mold, govern, direct, organize, modulate, and determine *our experience in navigating* through the world. Since we do not deal with the world directly, but only through our maps, these neurological-linguistic maps govern our experiences. They determine what we can see or not see, what we feel or don't feel, how we organize our skills (or fail to do so), how we portray to ourselves (and others) our options and choices in the world, the programs that we build for coping and adapting, etc.

No wonder our paradigmatic models of the world carry so much influence in our lives! They become the *interface* between the real world "out there" and our subjective experience of that world. This means that **the "magic" occurs in knowing the leverage points for altering impoverishing maps**.

In **The Structure of Magic**, Bandler and Grinder first pointed us in the direction of **the linguistic markers** (distinctions) that indicate possible mapping problems that leave us feeling (or experiencing) the lack of choices and hence un-resourceful in coping. Via these linguistic markers (and other non-linguistic markers, *The Structure of Magic—Volume II*) we have pathways into a human reality structure (our constructed model of the world). By moving along these pathways, we have the opportunity to most effectively challenge impoverished maps, assist ourselves or another to re-connect to the deeper structures (the earliest abstractions we made from our experiences), and to remap in more enhancing ways.

The process of using the meta-modeling distinctions to address and overcome ill-formed maps offers us the **leverage points of transformation**. Or, if we shift to a computer analogy for a moment, we could say that the linguistic markers in the Meta-model which indicate various qualities and codings of our mental maps—these provide us *the human programming language*. Now, taking our mapping and maps into consideration, our experiences (perceptions, emotions, behaviors, psychosomatic illnesses, skills, etc.) begin to make more sense. Now also the experiences and "reality" of others makes more sense. Whatever behavior they produce makes perfect sense *given their mapping*.

Even what we call "dysfunctional" and pathological behavior makes perfect sense. Given a person's model of the world, how they then attempt to cope, respond, and navigate makes perfect sense. It may not work. It may not get them what they want. But in terms of their reality model and strategy—their responses makes sense. Further, if we modeled their way of thinking, reasoning, languaging, etc., we could replicate their "way of being" and experiencing the world.

This fits with what John and Richard repeatedly asserted in the early days of NLP, namely that "people are not broken, they work perfectly well."

The *broken model* of human psychology had it all wrong. Schizophrenics "are" not "crazy" in any ultimate sense—they just operate from a very different map from our maps. And further, the map that any given schizophrenic uses *works*. It works regularly, methodically, and systematically. You can count on it working with consistency and regularity. In other words, there is structure in their madness! The "black" magic that makes their lives a living hell makes perfect sense when we examine the content of their ideas, beliefs, understandings, etc.

Again, **the map controls the magic.** It always does. It does so due to the extent that human consciousness involves a languaged consciousness.

"Magic" As Wonderful Skills

Sometimes we use the term "magic" to refer to the absolutely amazing, incredible, and wonderful skills, abilities, and powers that we see exhibited in some people. When we encounter a highly talented artist, scientist, musician, therapist, educator, or anyone performing at what we call a "genius" level, we stand back and marvel in awe.

> "How can they perform with such high-level quality of achievement?"
> "What explains their intuitive genius?"
> "They seem so gifted and so natural in what they produce!"
> "What a wizard to just know how to do this—in coming up with these new insights!"

Yet if all human subjective experience operates from "structure" (hence, neuro-linguistic mapping), then if we have sufficient tools for modeling such excellence, and spend the time to do so, we will eventually discover the structure of such "magic." In NLP, **the domain of modeling excellence** precisely involves these things. It involves finding *the internal strategies* that people use to perform seemingly "magical" feats—

> Relating quickly and effectively with people
> Persuading and influencing
> Teaching and educating
> Creating and innovating new products
> Marketing and creating new markets
> Losing weight and maintaining it over time
> Parenting through the years with grace, love, and firmness
> Managing people in achieving business outcomes
> Inventing new models and ideas in physics, chemistry, engineering, etc.
> Etc.

These exist as *learned skills* that we *develop* as we learn to use our neurological "languages" [including our sensory-based "languages" (the VAK), as well as our linguistics]. To function in any domain, as a gymnast, rock climber, pilot, diplomat, scholar, musician, hypnotist, or whatever, necessitates ordering and structuring consciousness. This syntactical ordering empowers us with the ability to send our attention in a certain direction in a certain way noticing particular qualities and filtering out others.

It also involves a semantical structuring. This refers to how the gymnast, rock climber, etc. languages him or herself in terms of beliefs, values, and identity. Having worked several years as a coach of boys' gymnastics and as a psychological consultant to a girls' team, I have come to understand firsthand some of the languaged distinctions that have to occur to turn a young person into a gymnast. The meta-level beliefs that support their intensely focused states involve certain Cause-Effect beliefs, Complex Equivalences, Identifications, etc. These include neuro-semantic constructions such as:

> "Only practice, practice, practice will turn me into a champion."
>
> "Falling and even getting hurt is just part of the process for becoming good."
>
> "I have what it takes to become a highly skilled gymnast."
>
> "Focusing all my attention totally and completely on my routine gives me more control."
>
> "I can see and feel my body going through the movements in my imagination."

What seems "magical" to an outsider in terms of the external structure of the experience seems common and "normal" to the one having the experience. Their model of the world represents this as their **reality strategy**.

Just prior to this writing, several Palestinian young men strapped on bombs, walked into a Jerusalem marketplace, and ignited them. What many of us would label as utterly strange and foreign "black magic"—unable to even imagine how they could do such (either to themselves or to their innocent victims), their comrades and associates would praise as the epitome of "white magic." Either way, the structure of such magic lies in the person's mapping processes—how they have syntactically learned to use their senses and how they have semantically learned to language their "reality."

"Magic" As Quick And Radical Changes

We also use the word "magic" in another way. We use it to refer to *a process that transforms so quickly and radically* that it violates our expectations and assumptions. In such instances, the process absolutely *shifts our paradigms* so that we have no explanatory model that explains the processes. It "blows our mind" and leaves us feeling stunned, overwhelmed, bamboozled!

> "I don't understand. How did you make my phobia just disappear?"
>
> "Amazing! Suddenly I don't feel bad at all when I think of things that way."
>
> "It took years and years for her to get that way—how could she just change like that?"
>
> "When you watch her work with clients—it seems like she just reaches right into their insides, tweaks a button or two, and, suddenly, they seem re-born into a new world. I don't get it."

This illustrates the powerful effect that systemic knowledge provides. Knowing where to intervene in a system of interactive parts, knowing where, when, and how to utilize the place where you can exercise the critical leverage point, appears as "magic" to an outsider. Sometimes we see this kind of "magic" with regard to mechanical things—cars, computers, televisions, VCRs, gadgets. Someone "in the know" about its engineering and structure can sometimes "tap" on a seemingly insignificant part and get the desired outcome in an instance.

A similar principle operates with regard to human functioning. If someone lets us in on the secret of our own design engineering (i.e. how to run our own brains), then suddenly the *structure of a phobia* no longer seems strange, foreboding, or incorrigible. "To have a phobia," whether we want to give one (!) or take one away from someone, we need to change the form and syntax of a person's internal representations. You can count on every phobia having a similar structure. When a person thinks (represents) a fear situation, he or she does it associatedly as if completely *in* the situation again. This representing, in turn, cues all of the autonomic nervous system defenses to respond as if threatened.

Simply by changing the coding to a "dissociated" set of representations the person's sense of threat immediately reduces. To step back to a meta-position of calm observing and then to an even calmer observing of that observer (to prevent a person from "stepping back into the horror movie") provides that individual with the ability to think *about* the fear, rather than the thinking *of it* (which occurs when the person steps into it). This spectator's viewpoint of the phobia now creates an expanded frame of reference. It allows the person to access other resources: calmness, relaxation, reality testing, etc. By thus *bringing these resources to bear* on the phobia, a person alters his or her model of the world. This changes everything.

So does playing "the movie" to its end, and then on to a scene of comfort. This provides process instructions about *where* to send one's attention—to a *scene of comfort*. To then step into that *comfort* and to associatedly rewind the movie in a fast rewind motion—while *inside* "the movie"—invites a person to experience an entirely different syntax. Running our knowledge backwards alters the meanings that we attribute to the meaning. And doing the one-second rewind of the phobia movie from inside repeatedly (five times or more) begins to habituate conscious attention to create a new syntax.

What a leverage point for transforming a phobic response! Who would have ever thought that such a procedure would have that kind of pervasive alteration? Psychologists for decades had assumed an entirely different theoretical basis for the "curing" of a phobia. They postulated that people had become fixated on the phobic object as a transform from some other fear and so sought to "analyze" it for years. Behaviorists eventually sped the process up to possibly six months using a re-conditioning process of gradual de-sensitization by training a neurological response of relaxing in the face of a noxious or toxic element.

Neuro-Linguistic Magic In Subjective States

This neuro-linguistic model of human functioning (i. e., thinking-emoting, speaking, behaving, and relating) gives us the secrets for understanding and installing **the structure of subjective experiences.** It provides us with the *magic* of marvelous skills and abilities. These include the strategies of genius—they also include the strategies of pathology. Here Bandler and Grinder established *a different attitude* from what we typically find in the field of psychology and psychotherapy. They did not look upon such subjective states as schizophrenia, multiple personalities, or phobias as inherently "bad" or "evil" experiences. They rather looked upon them as *human achievements.*

Using this *achievement frame*, they began to explore the structural and engineering questions. They asked, **How does this experience work**? Once they modeled it in terms of strategy, meta-programs, Meta-model distinctions, physiology, etc., they began to ask various utilization questions:

> What can we use it for?
> When and where would we find it a valuable strategy?
> How could we fine tune it to offer a useful skill?
> Where does the leverage point lie for transforming it?

People already in the field of psychology and psychotherapy didn't even have these questions in their paradigm. They began from the assumption that any and every pathology was "bad." This therefore prevented them from even asking such utilization questions. But for modelers from outside the paradigm who came into this arena of *human functioning*, and who didn't know to think of these as "bad" things, they used their *different attitude.* From that different attitude they asked different questions which, in turn, led them to move into an entirely different direction.

In 1982, Richard Bandler worked with a young schizophrenic named Andy before a videocamera. Richard related how Andy hallucinated "Mary" of the Mary on "Little House on the Prairie" TV series and how she would come off the screen and chase him around the house and "rag" on him with her little bitchy voice. "And," as Richard said, "he was a paranoid schizophrenic." Given that model of the world, it made sense.

According to Richard, when he first met with Andy, he adopted a different attitude from that held by the psychiatrists who worked with him. Rather than viewing it as a bad thing, Richard viewed it as a *human achievement*. Further, he didn't let the *content* throw him. When he found out that Andy hallucinated characters coming off the television and chasing him around, Richard asked, "What do you watch?" Upon hearing about the specific character who came off the TV and chased him, Richard said that he considered this "a million dollar disorder."

Why? Because he started thinking about other shows and channels—the Playboy channel, the Money channel, the History channel, etc. "We could teach this strategy to traveling salesmen so that they would never have to feel lonely again. But first, I want the strategy."

Richard then noted a change in Andy's response. From a guy who had worked for years to *not* have this experience and who had therapists trying to get him to *not* have those hallucinations, he went to a guy who responded to Richard's request for him to tell him **how** he did it with, "Well, maybe I'll tell you and maybe I won't."

This underscores the importance of **structure** over content. Yet getting hung up in content, especially in judging it as "good" or "bad" had blinded other theorists from even seeing, at the meta-level, the **form** of the mapping.

When Bandler and Grinder discovered *the structure* of the subjective experience of phobias, schizophrenia, or genius, it then became easy to mess them up and to transform them. Sometimes they could do so in just a matter of a few minutes. They then applied this phobia cure model to enabling a person to recover from tormenting internal memories about past traumas. "Memory," they recognized, simply describes our ongoing coding of past events. Change the internal representations of those events, and the meta-level meanings given to it, and we change the experience of ongoing traumatization.

The ongoing discovery of **the structure of magic** continues today whenever we look upon all forms of human behavior, skills, and responses as accomplishments. Starting from that perspective and attitude, we can then go after the internal **strategy** by which it operates. This means learning to identify, articulate, and specify the strategies that empower people for effectiveness in all kinds of realms that express their personal genius (e. g. communicating and relating, selling and persuading, parent and bonding, accessing states of creativity, etc.). In terms of working with maladaptive strategies that create pain and limitations, it involves a similar strategy analysis.

The Magic Of Modeling

Thus we return to the place where NLP began—*modeling*. It brings us back to the modeling attitude:

> How does this process work?
> What internal structure governs the way this experience works?
> What does a person represent first, then second, then third, etc.?
> What other qualities and factors play a crucial role in the formula of this piece of human excellence?
> If I took your place for a day so that you could have a day off from this problem, teach me how to do it.

As magic continued in the history of NLP, Robert Dilts along with Bandler and Grinder and Judith DeLozier put together a formative work, *NLP: The Study of the Structure of Subjective Experience, Volume I*. This 1980 work summarized the NLP "strategy" model by rehearsing the modeling process from the beginning conceptions of thinking of human subjectivity as a rule-governed structure. Using representational systems as the language of strategies, they prescribed processes for identifying strategies, unpacking strategies, eliciting strategies, etc.

Since that time, numerous NLP works have followed which have presented specific strategies for excellence in sports, education, management, law, health, medicine, therapy, and many other fields. Here the idea of "magic" (or human excellence that amazes and astonishes the uninitiated) has extended far beyond the field of psychotherapy.

Conclusion

The "magic" of NLP focuses primarily on empowering people to find and develop more resources in life for accomplishing things of value. It offers the "magic" of using one's mind-and-body in a balanced way to create the richest kind of maps for navigating reality. It offers the "magic" of reframing the meanings that we give to things, people, events, and words so that we always have a sense of choice and response-ability.

Chapter 6

Conversational Magic

"Sleight Of Mouth" Reframing

"Words are the physicians of a mind diseased."
(Aeschylus)

When we first learn the Meta-model, we typically embark upon a slow and laborious task. We look again at *language usage* itself—nouns, verbs, adjectives, adverts, pronouns, prepositions, etc. We review its structure, syntax, and level of specificity. Some find this reminiscent of school days when they first made grammar and language use conscious. They experienced such as confusing, boring, stressful, etc. Set such grammar studies about how to punctuate and describe the structure of language hardly seems very "magical," does it?

Yet, as with any science or art, this one too first demands that we become a detailed technician and so we methodically go through the "lessons." We earn our right to our degree in "magic" by putting in the time, energy, and trouble as we do the drills, learn the "chops," and practice it until it becomes ... unconscious again. Thus we move from *unconscious incompetence*—we don't know that language works its magic nor how (incompetence), and we don't even know that we don't know. Then we become conscious of our incompetence. "Hey, this is hard! Why do I have to learn this stuff? What does verbs, nouns, nominalizations, unspecified referential indices, and all of this other crap have to do with magic?" [At the stage of conscious incompetence we usually complain and fuss a lot!]

Then slowly, as we become more and more competent, we attain higher and higher degrees of competency, skill, understanding, and awareness. The discipline of the field now becomes actually enjoyable. We begin to have conscious fun meta-modeling ourselves and others! We begin to delight ourselves in the experience of seeing how to play with words in new ways.

As this continues, our progress moves us into higher levels of mastery. And with mastery, we eventually become unconscious again. Then unconscious competence manifests itself as just an in-knowing (or "intuition") about it all. Now we can do it conversationally while engaged in other things even more exciting—like picking up on and modeling various forms of human excellence.

Conversational Reframing

The NLP model has a set of patterns for reframing someone's neuro-linguistic reality of beliefs, ideas, feelings, attitudes, etc. We call this domain "The Sleight of Mouth Patterns." These presuppose a masterful competence with the Meta-model and with the principle of reframing (putting an idea or representation in another frame of reference). Here a person simply responds **conversationally** to the semantic ill-formedness that comes out in everyday expressions. Rather than meta-modeling, we redirectionalize consciousness and offer various responses that stream-line the process.

Picking up on the analogy of a quick-hand artist who pulls *"Sleight of Hand" maneuvers* at an amusement park, the so-called "magic" occurs by mis-directing attention. The artist misdirects attention by setting the frame for his or her audience by saying, "The hand is quicker than the eye." To this "come on," the observers decide to really "look" and to look faster and harder than ever so that no hand will trick their eye!

This rigidity of focus in the observers, however, plays into the artist's "sleight of hand" movements. It allows him or her to make moves at other places—without being noticed.

This principle holds true for *the "Sleight of Mouth" patterns.* While we seemingly keep attention on whatever the person said—at other levels and directions we shift frames. Yet typically, they never notice. They just accept the frame and therefore buy into it as a given without question. And whoever sets the frame—governs the subsequent thoughts, feelings, behaviors, and experiences (a basic meta-level presupposition).

Mind-Lines: **Lines** *For Changing* **Minds**

In a recent work on which I collaborated with Bob Bodenhamer (1997), we reworked, updated, and expanded the NLP "Sleight of Mouth" patterns. We rigorously applied this pattern to a logical level system. Doing this we discovered that we could specify **seven directions for directionalizing attention.** This then led to identifying **twenty** different patterns within the seven directional classes. We titled these patterns **Mind-Lines**—lines to "magically" change minds via conversational reframing. [The following comes directly from Chapter 1 of *Mind-Lines*.]

Language Patterns—Using Them To Make A Difference

The Meta-model, as an explanatory model for how language works in neurology to construct our sense of "reality," enables us to easily see how language patterns play such a relevant and inescapable role in all areas of life. Language governs the workings and health of families, businesses, churches, schools, political parties, and social environments. Language creates or destroys and enhances or limits life in these systems.

The NLP language patterns truly offer a gold mine of opportunity for us to enrich our lives. These language patterns provide more understanding about how we affect life in such systems by the way we talk and the symbols we use. By extending our maps with these language patterns we experience more behavioral flexibility. This, in turn, expands our skills and powers of persuasion, influence, clarity, etc.

The importance of language is indicated by the fact that our language both describes and reflects our model of the world. Our languaging reflects how we have built our mental maps by the modeling processes of deletion, generalization, and distortion from our neu*rological* representations of what we have seen, heard, felt, etc.

What importance does this hold for us if we want to do *Conversational Magic?* Much.

Ultimately, the secret in moving a person in a desired direction involves languaging that person in such a way so that they will signal their own mind-body to represent things in a certain way. The NLP communication model specifies two kinds of conversational magic. One involves *chunking up* to higher levels of abstraction and *chunking down* to levels of greater precision.

1. The Language Of Specificity For Precision And Clarity

Consider the following sensory-based illustration. Imagine it as a rebuke that a mother might say to a youngster,

> "Would you turn around (K) and look (V) at the dirt on the carpet that have the shape of your footprints. Now what do you have to say (A) about that?"

Did that clearly communicate? Go with that description for a moment to "experience" the words. Follow the language as *instructions*. Begin with "turn around" and "look," etc. You may not have carpet under your feet. If not, then pretend that you do. You may not be standing at this very moment and yet you can imagine yourself standing. You may not be standing inside a room, but again, you can pretend. To "influence" you to signal your brain to run this movie—which you've done already (have you not?)—I only needed to provide you *clear specific symbols.* Your brain took those symbols and turned them into neuro-linguistic reality—even if only for a moment.

Similarly, for you to invite another person to move their internal representation in a specific direction, you get them to make a movie that corresponds to the one in your head. Do this by simply describing to that person (or client) what you see, hear, sense, and say inside your head. Simple? Yes—in a way. And in another way—not so simple.

And why, pray tell, could we not find this "simple?"

Because most people don't know how to talk in sensory-based terms! We have done what humans all over the planet do all too well and too quickly, we have "gone meta" into higher levels of abstraction and so we talk in non-sensory based terms.

"You are so rude to come into my clean house and make a filthy mess. I get so angry at your irresponsibility."

Ah, a different kind of confrontation from the former one, don't you think?

[By the way, this illustrates an extremely powerful NLP technology. If you need to say something unpleasant or "confrontative" (ah another nominalization!)—you can say almost anything to anybody if you use sensory-based descriptive language. And, you can say almost nothing to anybody if you use evaluative, non-sensory based language!]

When we abstract up from *sensory based words* (first level of *linguistic languaging*) to greater and greater levels of *non-sensory based language*, we move into increasingly levels where "thought" goes abstract. As language becomes more **abstract** we delete more of the specific sensory information and **generalize** to a higher level. Thus we create a model of reality via these symbolic processes. Now this enables us to say or write things such as this:

"Objective consideration of contemporary phenomena compels the conclusion that success or failure in competitive activities exhibits no tendency to be commensurate with innate capacity, but that a considerable element of the unpredictable must invariably be taken into account."

Did you like that? Thank George Orwell (1950, Shooting an Elephant and Other Essays) for that one. Sounds abstract, right? Sounds "intellectual," right? But did you go, "What in the world does he mean with all of that?" Ah, the danger of abstractions. Too much nominalization (as in that sentence) and the deletions, generalizations, and distortions (the three modeling processes, which we will present more fully later) leaves us so high up the scale of abstraction that we can get lost in the ozone. (Of course, some people live there most of the time!)

Would you like to see the original piece from which Orwell made that "intellectual" abstraction? Here it goes,

> *"I returned and saw under the sun that the race is not to the swift, nor the battle to the strong, neither yet bread to men of understanding, nor yet favor to men of skill; but time and chance happeneth to them all."* (Ecclesiastes 9:11)

While we have some nominalizations in that one (especially "time"), it basically presents a sensory-based description of events that one can see-hear-and-feel. It offers us symbols whereby we can more easily signal our "mind" about what to represent. We can make a movie out of those words without much trouble. Our point? When we "go meta" to a higher logical level of symbolization and use more abstract words (nominalizations, class words, etc.), we use a different kind of *representational system*, a non-sensory based modality. We call this higher-level abstraction *auditory-digital* (A_d) in NLP. And because we can continue the process of saying more words about words, we can create ever more abstract words and language forms.

We really, really enrich our language and communication when we use more and more *specific* visual, auditory, kinesthetic, and sensory-based language components about the movie we have constructed within our head. Re-read the Orwell passage quoted above and the biblical referent that it translates. Which makes more sense? Which do you find easier to understand? Notice all of the sensory-based language referents in the original text from Ecclesiastes and contrast to the abstractions and generalizations in the "modern" translation. Though the modern "translation" sounds more intellectual—it lacks the power of precision and clarity.

So to communicate with more clarity and precision, **go descriptive.** The words will flow out of your mouth as you describe what you actually experience and represent, and hence what you wish for the one with whom you communicate. Without the ability to distinguish between *descriptive* and *evaluative* language forms, you will never become truly professional or elegant in your language use. When you begin to learn the power and simplicity of see-hear-feel language (sensory-based language), you provide yourself a magic wand—*the magic wand of clarity.*

2. Use The Language Of Evaluation To Construct "Realities"

"Should we therefore never use abstract or non-sensory based language?"

"Of course not."

Such language represents our uniqueness and glory as human beings. We only need to do so with more *mindfulness*, thoughtfulness, and "consciousness of abstracting."

Here NLP provides a wonderful model and tool for guiding our understanding of **what we do with words,** and the effect our languaging has on ourselves and others.

Many times, instead of getting a person to accurately and specifically represent (or cue their brain) with certain VAK signals, we need to move them to a higher logical level—and offer them new abstractions that will *set a whole new frame of reference* for them.

Using such language *constructs* new "realities" as it creates new meanings.

Sometimes this moves a person from one position at a meta-level to another level. For instance, suppose a father sees his teenage son lying on the couch watching TV. Here we have a sensory-based set of representations. Or did you already draw a conclusion and evaluate it? Suppose the father sees such and immediately jumps up a logical level and classifies that behavior as a member of the class of "laziness." The nominalization "laziness" represents his **frame of reference** for making sense (meaning) of the VAK event. He looks at the specific behaviors and does not see them as mere sensory-based pieces of information. He looks and sees *Laziness* with a capital L. Right?

Yet "laziness" does **not** exist in the world. No nominalization exists "out there." What exists in the world? Only the see-hear-feel information: lying on a couch, watching TV, turning over slowly, etc. The **meanings** that we (as meaning-makers) give to those VAK signals depends upon our *beliefs, values, understandings, abstractions, frames-of-references, etc.* (The meta-level phenomena). Some parents may look at the same signals and, using *other* frames, may say:

"I'm so glad John can relax and enjoy the good things of life, unlike my traumatic childhood, and I'm so thrilled that I can provide for him all the things I never had."

It could happen!

Meaning (semantics) exists only, and exclusively, in the "mind." It exists and arises as *a form of evaluation and appraisal*, hence, a higher logical level abstraction *about* the information. It exists as information-about-information, thoughts at a higher level (meta-level) *about* lower level signals. The term *neuro-semantic* truly describes these higher levels, in contradistinction to *neuro-linguistic* for the primary level of sensory-based descriptions.

[Yes, this represents an arbitrary definition. It does, however, provide an important distinction between the associations and meanings that we experience at the primary level when consciousness goes out to recognize and represent the world and when consciousness comes back onto itself to have thoughts about its thoughts.]

In **reframing,** we essentially do a horizontal shift at the meta-level that essentially says,

> *"This doesn't mean this—it means this."*
> *"Not X, but Y."*

"John isn't being lazy. He simply really knows how to relax and enjoy himself."
"Jill isn't rude. She just forgot to wipe her feet."
"Jerry isn't ugly and hateful. He has just gotten into a very unresourceful state and feels really threatened."
"Terri isn't trying to put you down. She just feels overwhelmed and has become emotionally preoccupied with three little ones and the recent death of her mother."

In the language patterns (or **mind-lines**) that follow, we have numerous ways to reframe meanings. And such *reframing trans-forms meaning*. These linguistic mind-line patterns provides resourceful ways *to put the best frame-of-reference on things so that we can operate more effectively.*

Figure 6:1

Diagram Of The Reframing Model

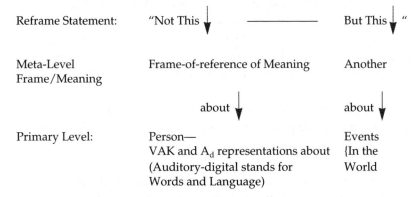

unused

| Reframe Statement: | "Not This | ——————— | But This " |

Meta-Level   Frame-of-reference of Meaning   Another
Frame/Meaning

about ↓   about ↓

Primary Level: Person—   Events
                   VAK and A_d representations about   {In the
                   (Auditory-digital stands for   World
                   Words and Language)

3. Use Evaluation-Of-Evaluation Language
To Construct High Level Meanings

Another form of reframing involves making a vertical move (going up) rather than moving horizontally. When we do this, we leave the frame-of-reference at the first level the same, and move to a higher level, and from there **outframe** the whole context. We create a new context for the context. ("Outframe" here refers to setting up a frame-of-reference **over** everything that lies underneath it.)

Suppose, for illustration, we talk at the primary level about a person who signals his brain with all kinds of VAK and A_d (words) cues of getting a physical beating with a stick when a child for simply acting and thinking like a kid. "You stupid brat, you'll never succeed in life with that attitude!" "What's wrong with you—are you an idiot?" Got the picture? Not very pretty, huh?

Now suppose the kid (let's call him Wayne) grows up and makes several beliefs from those experiences. Suppose he concludes the following:

> "I'll never amount to anything."
> "Something's wrong with me. I must be defective because I have this 'attitude.'"
> "I don't feel very loved or loveable, therefore I must not be loveable."

With **evaluative meanings** like that, guess what kind of neuro-semantic states Wayne will continually create for himself as he moves through life? Certainly not the most resourceful. These states would likely only reinforce and deepen his psychological distresses—giving him more "proof" of his internal mapping. So as he grows and receives more of the same, he draws another, even higher meta-level frame of reference,

> "I'll never change. This is the way life is going to be. No need to get my hopes up that things will turn around. I'm just a loser and always will be."

That neuro-semantic state, as a state-about-state (hence a *meta-state*), will then *multiply* his psychological pain and create even more of a self-fulfilling prophecy. It *sets the frame* for his lower states. It becomes a meta-level belief that will organize experience under it. With that belief working at a meta meta-level, reframing Wayne at the first meta-level will not have much effect. So if you do a reframe,

> "It's not that you won't amount to anything, it's that you started with a handicap that we need to change."

That reframe probably won't work. Because at a higher logical level, another frame exists to discount it.

> "No kidding I started with a handicap. But as we all know, 'You can't teach old dog new tricks.' So don't give me any of your psychobabble crap!"

In this case, we need to **outframe beyond** Wayne's highest outframe. So, we go up and find the meta meta-frame, and then go *above* that frame and set a whole new frame of mind.

"So those are the ideas and beliefs you built as an eight-year old boy and then on top of that, at 17 you built that stuck-and-can't change belief." ["Yeah, so?"] "And now here you are at 30 living out these old beliefs—how well do you like those beliefs? Do they serve you very well?" ["No, not at all."] "So the conclusions you drew at 8 and 17 don't work very well. Well, that's probably the best kind of thinking that the younger you could do at those times. Yet, after all, they do reflect the thinking of a child, not a grown man who can step back from it and look back on all that and recognize them as misbeliefs and erroneous conclusions, can you not? Because children tend to do self-blame rather than recognize that their parents didn't take or pass *'Parenting 101'* and know how to affirm or validate..."

Figure 6:2
Diagram Of Reframing With The Meta-Model

Meta *Meta* Meta-Level
New Enhancing Frame-of-Reference *"Not This frame* ⁄ *But This higher frame* ⁄*"*
that outframes the lower frames....
that **Outframes**

Meta Meta-level
Frame/Meaning that Sets the frame
on a previous frame

Meta-Level   Frame-of-reference of Meaning   Another Frame/Meaning
                   about ↓   about ↓

Primary Level: Person—VAK and A_d representations about⟶   X

Framing And The Creation Of Meaning
(Deframing, Reframing, Outframing, Preframing, Postframing, etc.)

In using the language of *mind-lines* to alter our "reality" (or someone else's) which then transforms external expressions (emotions, behaviors, speech, skill, relationships, etc.), we will play with their **frames.** (Yes, we all have frames!) *Frames* (as in frames-of-reference) refers to the content references that we use or the cognitive domains within which we embed our ideas.

Neuro-linguistic and neuro-semantic reality begin not with the world as such, but with our **thoughts** *about* such. Apart from our thoughts, *nothing means anything.* Apart from our thoughts, only events occur. Things happen. Sights, sounds, sensations, etc.

stimulate our sense receptors. Then the magic begins. We see, hear, and feel such and so *represent* it and *connect* (or associate it) with other sights, sounds, and sensations, and then later, connect to it even higher level abstractions. Thus **we give it meaning.**

First level meaning involving *giving or attributing meaning to something* (to anything) involves an associative process. We link the external event, action, or behavior up with some internal representation or thought. Sounds simple enough, right?

Not!

This seemingly simple and obvious linkage begins the creation of "meaning." What does anything mean anyway?

What does "fire" *mean?* It all depends upon what any given individual (or animal) has connected, linked, or associated with it. This sends us back to **experiences.** Have we seen and experienced fire only as campfires when camping, and associated with food, marshmallows, companionship, etc.? Then the **external behavior** (EB) of "fire" *means* (relates to, causes, connects up with, etc.) the **internal state** of fun, delight, joy, togetherness, attraction, excitement, etc.

How very very different for the person whose experience of "fire" relates to getting burned, feeling physical pain, seeing a home destroyed, etc. What does "fire" mean to that person? Again, it all depends on what that person (conceptually and mentally) has connected to, and associated, with "fire." For that person, "fire" probably *means* hurt, pain, loss, grief, aversion, etc.

So what does "fire" *really* mean? (Get ready for a surprise.) It "really" "means" **nothing.** Fire only exists as a certain event of change in the external world. Alone—unconnected by and to consciousness—it has no meaning. Nothing has any inherent meaning. Meaning only and exclusively arises when a consciousness comes along and connects a thing to an internal reference. Then we have a *frame-of-reference.* We might have "fire" seen, heard, felt, and languaged from the frame of a campfire or from a home burning down.

In either case—**the frame completely and absolutely controls the meaning.** In fact, we cannot even understand the EB (external behavior or event) *apart from* the frame. Apart from the frame, we don't know anything about its meaning to another person. Apart from knowing their frame—we tend to use our frames-of-references and so impose our meanings upon them.

So what do we have? We have two major factors, one external, the other internal. The external component: Events. The internal component: a nervous system taking cognizance of the event. (Cognizance means awareness.) We cognize the event via our sensory-system languages: visual sights (V), auditory sounds (A), kinesthetic sensations (K), olfactory smells (O), and gustatory tastes (G) as well as by our digital language system of words (Ad).

These two phenomena occur at different levels and in different dimensions. But when we connect them, we have suddenly created neuro-linguistic meaning/magic. In *formula format* we have:

External Behavior = Internal State

This creates the basic *frame-of-reference* that we use to attribute meaning to things. It explains how not only humans make meaning, but how animals can also experience and develop associative learning and understandings. *Things get connected to things.* Things of the outside world (events, behaviors) get associated with internal feelings, moods, states, ideas, understandings, values, etc. When they do—we develop "beliefs."

Once we have a frame (as in the above formula: EB=IS), we don't stop there. Animals generally do, but not us humans. No way. We have a special kind of consciousness that can *reflect back onto itself* (self-reflexive consciousness). So whenever we have a thought, "I like fire; it makes me feel warm and loved." "I hate fire. Fire is scary; it makes me shudder just to think about it.", we never leave it there. We then complicate matters (wouldn't you know it?) by then *having a thought about that thought!* "I hate it that I fear fire so much." Nor do we leave it alone at that level, we bring even more thoughts to bear on the thoughts, etc. This describes second-level meaning processes—contexts and contexts of contexts.

> "Why do I let fire frighten me so much. I should get over this thing. What's wrong with me anyway that I can't be more reasonable? Well, I guess I'm stuck for life. Once you've had a traumatic experience like that, it seals your fate."

Now we have a real neuro-semantic muddle, do we not? To the original relations and connections that the person made with fire, he or she has *layered* more and more abstract ideas to it. This creates not only beliefs, but belief systems, then belief systems about belief systems, etc. Or, to use the metaphor of a frame, the thoughts that we bring to bear on our earlier thoughts, set up a frame-of-reference around a frame, and then a frame around that frame, etc.

Frames-Of-Frames

Once we have a basic frame established (EB=IS), then we can set a frame *above that* frame (a meta-frame or an out-frame). Or we could set a frame-of-reference (thoughts) about it *prior* to it. Parents do this for kids regarding experiences (events) yet to come, "Now don't *fall into the fire*—that would be terrible!" In addition to pre-framing, we can frame events and behaviors afterwards (post-framing). "Yep, sonny, if you burned yourself in a fire once, you are likely to do it again and again!" How do you like that post-frame as a way of thinking? Pretty shoddy and muddled thinking, right? (This also will typically operate as a "post hypnotic suggestion.")

We can de-frame by undermining the EB=IS formula. Asking specific questions about either the EB or the IS tends to pull apart the thought-construction (belief, meaning equation).

"When did you get burned?" "In what circumstances?" "What did you learn from that?" "Have you used that learning to not repeat that experience?"

We can even do some fancy kind of mental gymnastics with our thought equation. We can, for example, *counter*-frame. We can ask or suggest experiences that stand counter to the EB=IS equation.

"Have you ever been around a campfire and enjoyed cooking a hotdog over the fire?" "How fearful and worried do you get when you strike a match and light candles on a birthday cake?"

These frames-of-frames provide numerous additional ways to reframe. We not only have to stay inside our magical belief/meaning box (thank God!), we can step outside that box and send our consciousness (or someone else's) in one or more of several directions. We can go *down* below the box and ask specific questions of the qualities of our modality representations (and the submodality qualities of those). Doing this deframes.

Or, we can **reframe** by going in one of two horizontal directions. We can go over to the left to a time *prior* to the frame-of-reference (the EB=IS formula) and **preframe** the subsequent response. Or, we can go over to the right to a time later than the basic first level meaning, and **postframe** it as meaning or suggesting something new and different.

Or, we can move up and **outframe** as we set up a whole new frame-of-reference with a thought-about-that thought. This then steps outside of the frame or context and generates a whole new context, a context-of-a-context.

Learning to make these conceptual shifts gives us the ability to use various **mind-lines** to alter neuro-linguistic and neuro-semantic realities. This process expands our sense of choice. It gives us a sense that we have so many options about our *meaning attributions*. This develops and expands our sense of flexibility of mind, emotion, and language. Language patterning skills enrich our communication skills, making us more effective and professional, more elegant in persuasion, and more influential. (This preframes you for this study, if you didn't notice.)

Figure 6:3

The Directions Of Meaning

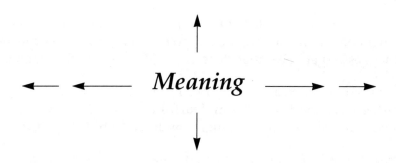

The Mind-Lines Model

This **directionalizing** and **re-directionalizing** of consciousness, sending it out in new and different ways so that we construct new and different meanings—empowering meanings that frame our experiential lives so that it makes us more resourceful, insightful, wise, thoughtful, etc.—summarizes the neuro-semantic process called "Sleight of Mouth" patterns. I prefer to call them **mind-lines**.

By **mind-lines** I refer to the fact that the *lines* (the linguistic constructions) that we connect and associate to things, that create our meaning formulas (EB=IS) exist as *mental constructs that have tremendous neurological effects*. As we change the lines that we use in our minds (and those we use on the minds of others), we transform "reality." We, at least, transform neuro-semantic reality. By the changing of meaning, our emotions change, as do our behaviors, habits, moods, attitudes, skills, health, etc. and our very life.

The following chart provides an overview of the *seven basic mind-shifting directions and the twenty different mind-line patterns for reframing reality.*

Chart 6:4

The Mind-Line Model
Twenty Ways To Reframe The Magic Box

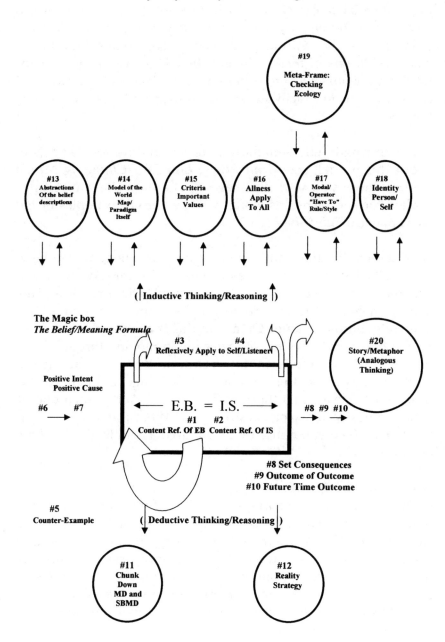

Reframing As The Tool For Mind-Lining

The "mental," cognitive, and conceptual shifting of meaning can take **seven basic directions**. Each direction (backward, forward, down, up, counter, etc.) offers us a different way to *directionalize consciousness*. By sending (or swishing) someone's "mind-and-emotion" in one of these different directions, we open up space for them (or ourselves) to experience new *frames-of-references that* can empower and facilitate greater resourcefulness, health, joy, love, etc.

The following briefly summarizes the seven directions. For more about this model, see **Mind-Lines: Lines for Changing Minds** (1997). There you will find several chapters that more fully explain these dimensions along with numerous examples of the word magic of *mind-lines*.

As a self-exploration, notice what frame-of-reference you have used in the last few moments as you have read this? What kind of a mental frame have you accessed and used? Did you use a "This is overwhelming!" frame? Some people might have used a "Too many big words!" frame? Or, a "Oh this is complicated!" frame? A "Oh boy, mind-lines to empower me in moving through life!" frame? A "I find this very interesting and wonder about the exciting ways to use this!" frame? A "One page and pattern at a time and I'll learn this thoroughly" frame? Well, which one of those frames would work best for you? What frame would you like to use? (Did you notice that I just used a couple of mind-*lines* on you!)

1. Content Reframing. We begin reframing in the center of the chart at the heart of **meaning**—in the box of meaning—where we find the complex equivalences and cause-effect statements. These *meaning equations and attributions* define the heart of neuro-semantic reality. Here we shift the meaning associations, "It doesn't mean this. It means this." This entails various facets of *content reframing*. In content reframing, we say, "Don't think that about this thing, event, act, etc., in that old way. Think about it in this new way."

> #1 Reframe EB
> #2 Reframe IS

2. Counter Reframing. Next we move to offer a reframe that *counters the content*. Here we let our consciousness reflect back onto its own content (the ideas within the meaning box) and apply the meaning equation to the other side of the equation to see if it coheres or if that breaks it up and deframes it. This easy to do reframing process involves what we call "reflexivity" or self-reflexive consciousness—"mind" that can think about its own thoughts. In Counter Reframing, we ask, "What do you think of the belief when you apply it to yourself?" "What do you think of the belief when you apply it to those cases, times, and events, where it does not fit?"

> #3 Reflexively Apply EB to Self/Listener
> #4 Reflexively Apply IS to Self/Listener
> #5 Counter-Example

3 and 4. Pre-and Post-Framing. In these conceptual moves we reframe by moving to (in our minds, of course) the prior state or a post state to the meaning construction (the formula in the box) and then "run with the logic" to see if the meaning equation makes sense. Does the magic still work?

This introduces "time" reframing as we play around with the "time" frame that surrounds the *meaning box*. Here we bring various "time" conceptualizations (thoughts) to bear upon our belief-thoughts in the meaning box. In Pre-Framing, we say, "Put this thought in the back of your mind." Whereas in Post-Framing, we say, "Keep this thought in the front of your mind about that belief as you move into your future." Again, this challenges the magic in the box.

Before Time:	#6 Positive Prior Framing or Intention
	#7 Positive Prior Cause
After Time:	#8 First Outcome
	#9 Outcome(s) of Outcomes
	#10 Eternity or Ultimate Framing

5. Deframing. We next move to chunking-down the meaning equation by pulling apart the component pieces of the VAK and A_d that make up the belief. The chunking-down movement involves deductive thinking/reasoning processes. In Deframing, we say, "Undermine your mind by thinking of all the specifics that lie underneath the belief." This shift helps us to de-think (to de-stabilize our belief thoughts) as we analyze the magic and see it evaporate.

> #11 Chunk Down on EB or IS
> #12 Reality Strategy Chunk Down

6. Outframing to meta-levels. We then move to chunk up the meaning construction to higher and higher levels of concept, bringing new and different facets to bear on our neuro-semantic construction. All of these chunking-up moves involve inductive thinking/reasoning processes. In Outframing, we say, "Wrap your mind around the belief in this way." Frequently, these moves not only challenge the old magic, but bring new and higher magic to bear on the belief.

> #13 Abstracting the EB or IS
> #14 Model of the World Framing
> #15 Criteria/Value Framing
> #16 Allness Framing
> #17 Have-To Framing
> #18 Identity Framing
> #19 Ecology Framing

7. Analogous Framing. Finally, we shift out of inductive and deductive thinking as well as horizontal and counter thinking, to analogous thinking (abduction, Bateson, 1972). We do this by shifting to storytelling, metaphor, and narrative. In this abducting type of framing, we essentially say, "Forget that, and let me tell you a story..."

> #20 Metaphoring/ Storying and
> Restorying Framing

The following offer a couple of examples of these mind-lines in action up against some idea or belief system that fails to empower.

Twenty Ways To Reframe "Failure"

The Toxic Thought:
"Whenever I don't succeed, it really bothers me. It makes me feel like a failure. I just hate not reaching my goals for that purpose."

Formula – the Toxic Magic
"Don't reach a goal" (EB) = "Feel like a failure" (IS)

1. Reframe The EB
The significance of not reaching your goal means that you have received information about numerous ways that will **not** get you there. Now you can feel free to explore new possible avenues.

2. Reframe The IS
Interesting that you say that. What I really find as a failure—and I mean failure with a big F –occurs when someone doesn't reach a goal and then just sits down in the dirt and quits, and won't learn or try again. I'd call that a failure.

3. Reflexively Apply To Self
Does that mean if you don't reach your goal in presenting this limiting and painful belief to me, that just talking to me will turn you into a failure?

4. Reflexively Apply To Listener
Then with that way of thinking about things, if I don't succeed in coming up with a good way of responding and helping you with this distress, I will become a big failure also! In other words, my success or failure as a human being depends on succeeding in this conversation in just the right way?

5. Counter-Example Framing
When you think about some of your successes and how good and resourceful you feel about them—you mean if you mispronounced a word, or failed in any aspect of any goal surrounding that, that such would turn you into a failure?

6. Positive Prior Intentional Framing
Reaching the goals that you set for yourself must mean a lot to you. I can imagine that you take that view in order to protect yourself from messing things up and for pushing yourself to higher levels. And since you want that, perhaps some other attitudes about failure might help you to really succeed in your goals.

7. Positive Prior Causation Framing
It seems important to you to set and reach goals. So you probably have taken on this limiting belief because you have had some painful experiences and you want to protect yourself against more pain. I wonder what other beliefs you could build that you would find more effective than this one?

8. First Outcome
What results for you when you move through life defining experiences and yourself as "failures" just because you don't reach a goal as you want to? Do these serve you well in setting and reaching goals or in feeling successful? Do you like those negative unresourceful feelings?

9. Outcome Of Outcome
Imagine going out, say five or even ten years from now, after you have defined every unsuccessful attempt at reaching a goal as turning you into a failure, and then living from that failure identity and feeling unresourceful... what will come out of that? Will you take as many risks? What other outcomes from feeling like a failure would probably result?

10. Eternity Framing

When I think about this I wonder what you will think when you look back on this belief about failure when you step over into eternity, and how you will think and feel about this limiting belief as you moved through life.

11. Chunking Down

As you think about something for which you define yourself as a failure, how do you represent this? What pictures, sounds, feelings, and words do you use? How do you represent the action of failing at one thing as "making" you a failure?

12. Reality Strategy Chunk Down

Since you seem to have bought into this way of viewing things, help me to understand this. How specifically does failing at one thing on a particular day make you a failure? What do you see first, then what do you say about that, and next?

13. Abstracting The EB Or IS

So as you think about not reaching a goal and labeling it as making you a "failure," I take it that you do this a lot? You take a specific instance and over-generalize it into a whole category? And you do this so successfully, don't you? Would you like to fail at this success?

14. Model Of The World Framing

What an interesting way to think about events and in overloading them with meaning! Do you know where you got this map about one unsuccess equalling failing? Do you know that most people don't use that map to torture themselves?

15. Criteria/Value Framing

When you think about your values of enjoying life, appreciating people, doing your best, etc., do you not think of those values as more important that making the "success/failure" judgment about every action?

16. Allness Framing

So since everybody has failed at something at some time in life, that must make everybody on this planet a failure!

17. Have-To Framing
What would it feel like for you if you did not evaluate events in terms of success or failure? What would happen if you didn't do that?

18. Identity Framing
What an interesting belief about your self-identity—so totally dependent on your behaviors. Do you know where you got this mental map? Did you install it yourself or did someone else?

19. Ecology Framing
How enhancing do you think this belief serves people just learning a new skill, trying a new sport, taking a risk and practicing a new social behavior? Would you recommend this belief as a way for them to succeed with greater ease and positive feelings? Does it empower or limit your endeavors?

20. Metaphoring/Storying And Restorying Framing
So the day that you brushed your hair but did not get every single hair on your head in just the right way that you wanted them, that also made you a failure?

When my daughter Jessica turned nine months, she began the process of learning to walk, but she couldn't walk upon the first attempt—nor upon the first hundred attempts. She constantly fell down. And she would sometimes cry. But most of the time she would just get up and try again. As she did, she developed more strength in her legs, and learned more about balance and movement, so that eventually she got the hang of it, and had a lot of fun in the process. And I wonder if this says anything that you can **take and apply to yourself now.**

Twenty Ways To Reframe "Learning Difficulty"

The Toxic Thought:
"I can't learn these mind-lines because they involve too much complexity about the structure of the language patterns."

Formula – the Toxic Magic
"Too much complexity" (EB) = "I can't learn" (IS)

1. Reframe The EB
How interesting! What I really find as truly complex and difficult to learn is the chaotic "word salad" that a schizophrenic produces… trying to find order and structure in that—now I'd call *that* difficult!

2. Reframe The IS
The problem may seem like you can't learn these language patterns, but don't you think that the real problem lies in how much effort you feel that you will have to expend to learn them? You can learn them, but the learning may not come as quickly and easily as you would like it too.

3. Reflexively Apply To Self
What? I don't understand. Why do you have to make such difficult and complex complaints? I just can't figure out what you really mean by these complicated complaints.

4. Reflexively Apply To Listener
Wow! That seems like a pretty complex analysis of your learning strategy! Where did you learn to think and reason in such a complex way?

5. Counter-Example Framing
So do you mean to tell me that you've never learned anything that once upon a time might have seemed complex to you? Somehow, the existence of complexity itself prevents you from learning?

6. Positive Prior Intentional Framing

How much awareness do you have that this belief about complexity protects you from failing to learn something new and exciting? And yet it also seems to protect you from taking on a mental challenge.

7. Positive Prior Causation Framing

So as you slow yourself down using this belief that complexity stops you from learning, it sounds like it enables you to move into new learning situations cautiously without tormenting yourself with high expectations that you need to learn too quickly or easily…

8. First Outcome

So if you use this belief and let it run your life, next year you will make no further progress in learning these language patterns. How does that work for you in terms of your communication and persuasion skills?

9. Outcome Of Outcome

As you imagine not learning anything about these mind-lines by next year, and remaining unskilled in them again the following year—what outcome will that lack of progress lead to? What will result from getting that result?

10. Eternity Framing

When you imagine stepping into eternity as you leave this world, and think about having backed off from learning—and especially from learning things that would improve your communication skills—how much do you think you will have missed out on life, relationships, and effectiveness by having let that complexity belief run your life?

11. Chunking Down

How do you know when to judge something as too "complex?" How do you represent "complex?" How do you know it exists as complexity and not just one layer of simple ideas upon another? How does the complexity stop you from learning altogether?

12. Reality Strategy Chunk Down

What leads you to first become aware of a complex subject? If you first see or say something to yourself, what do you then do? And what comes after that? How do you cue yourself that something has enough complexity to stop learning?

13. Abstracting The EB Or IS

How do you know that you should label this or that subject as "complex" and not just the next step in learning? What if you discovered that learning complexity actually involves the same mental processes as learning the foundational principles of a field? What if you discover that your labeling of a subject as having "complexity" itself creates the difficulty?

14. Model Of The World Framing

How interesting to posit learning as dependent upon complexity. Do you know where you got this map? From what experience did you map that difficult or layered subjects somehow prevent you from learning? How does it strike you when you realize that this merely comprises a map and not the territory?

15. Criteria/Value Framing

When you think about your value of growing and developing as a human being—how much more important does it feel to you when you think of the time and trouble you might need to take to learn a complex subject?

16. Allness Framing

Since everybody has encountered complex information at some time, does that mean that they cannot or should not attempt to learn such? Would you recommend this belief to other people? What would happen if everybody on the planet adopted this belief about complexity and learning?

17. Have-To Framing

What would it feel like if you did not operate from this belief that complexity stops or hinders learning?

18. Identity Framing

As you think about yourself as *a learner*, you certainly can think about some things that you have learned, piece by piece, and have learned so well, that when others look at it, they may conclude that you know some pretty complex things. What does that say about you?

19. Ecology Framing

As you think about believing that you can't learn complex things, how well does that belief serve you? Does it enhance your life? Does it increase your motivation and drive for learning? Does it increase your resilience? Would you recommend this belief to others?

20. Metaphoring/Storying And Restorying Framing

When I first saw a Hebrew text of the Bible, I thought, 'This is really a complex language. I don't know if I will ever learn this. 'Than I began to think about the children born to parents who speak Hebrew and how that they just grow up with that language, and that they learn it with as much ease and effectiveness as children in other language environments learn other languages.

Thinking about that made me realize the error in my conclusion about the so-called difficulty of Hebrew. I then realized that Hebrew isn't complex as much as simply different from what I already knew. So I began at the beginning. I first learned the shape and names of the Hebrew letters. I learned a little bit here and a little bit more there and eventually I gained a level of competency where I could read a page of a text. Yet what previously would have seemed so complex now seemed natural and easy—a piece of cake!

Conclusion

Based upon the formal understandings of the Meta-model—the *Sleight of Mouth* patterns emerge as ways that we can *conversationally frame and reframe* people (including ourselves). Doing this provides us with a way to engage in **conversational "magic"**—at least it frequently seems like and feels like "magic" to the recipient. Yet, as Bandler and Grinder originally noted, the "magic" has structure. It operates as rule-governed linguistic phenomena.

This means that as neuro-linguistic creatures, magic lies in the language that we use. It lies in the very structure of language itself. So the incantations that we create and use, on ourselves and others, operate according to neuro-linguistic principles. Knowing the structure of such neuro-semantic "magic" gives us a heightened skill in the effective use of enhancing "magic."

Chapter 7

Magic Beyond Words

Representational Magic
And
Emergent Magic From Multiple Maps

Until now, I have focused primarily on the structure of the "magic" that occurs in the meta-language of words. Yet NLP's *"the structure of magic"* does not only relate to the linguistic symbol system, it relates equally as well to *the non-linguistic systems*. In their second volume of *The Structure of Magic*, Bandler and Grinder identified other forms of "magic" in addition to the primary level linguistics. There they explored other representational systems (RS)—namely, the "language" of the senses (the VAK), the presence of multiple maps, and synesthesia mapping.

In examining the human modeling or mapping processes, they began with *Representational Systems (RS)* as "other maps for the same territory." These neurological maps of the sensory systems precede the linguistic maps, and so occur "before words."

Next, they looked at **the experience of incongruity**. This phenomenon arises from the experience of attempting to operate from *multiple models* of the world that conflict with each other. One facet (or part) of these models operates from one map while another part has abstracted another map and uses it.

Bandler and Grinder then turned to the domain of "Fuzzy Functions." They described these as cross-over circuits or **synesthesias**. In terms of mapping, this speaks about the interfacing of maps—how the input we get from one channel for a particular sensory map ends up getting coded and represented in another map. The way maps interface to create such fuzzy functions results in various subjective experiences—some heavens and others living hells.

Finally, they addressed the domain of multiple maps that arise in groups and families. As a systemic process, how do different models of the world interface within a family or between a couple?

To highlight these mapping processes, this chapter focuses on NLP technologies of "magic" that transcends words: the representational systems, anchoring, non-verbal pacing and leading, and "going meta" to operate at meta-levels using other symbols than words.

The Magical "Language" Of The Senses

One of the most surprising and profound developments in NLP arose from an area of the most sublime simplicity—*the sensory based awareness* that we experience and represent via our senses. Anthropologist Gregory Bateson noted this in his *Introduction* to *The Structure of Magic*.

> "We did not see that these various ways of coding—visual, auditory, etc.—are so far apart, so mutually different even in neurophysiological representation, that no material in one mode can ever be the same logical level in any material in any other mode. This discovery seems obvious when the argument starts from linguistics..." (pp. x-xi)

In the second volume of **The Structure of Magic**, Bandler and Grinder began with a chapter entitled, *"Representational Systems— Other Maps For The Same Territory."* There they introduced their discovery that words "work" in the human nervous system by evoking sensory-based representations—and that each of the senses exist itself as a **language system**. This means that the mapping processes (deletion, generalization, and distortion) that play such a crucial role in the Meta-model of propositional language also play as crucial a role in the sensory languages. In those systems also we delete, generalize, and distort the VAK information.

Thus underneath the language system lie other language systems—more primitive and basic.

- The Visual System
- The Auditory System
- The Kinesthetic System
- The Olfactory System
- The Gustatory System

Bandler and Grinder (1976) wrote,

> *"Human beings live in a 'real world.' We do not, however, operate directly or immediately upon that world, but, rather, we operate within that world using a map or a series of maps of that world to guide our behavior within it. These maps, or representational systems, necessarily differ from the territory that they model by the three universal processes of human modeling: Generalization, Deletion, and Distortion. When people come to us in therapy expressing pain and dissatisfaction, the limitations which they experience are, typically, in their representation of the world and not in the world itself."* (p. 3)

We create our **neurological maps** of the world as we use our sense receptors. The energy manifestations of the world (in the forms of waves, particles, etc.) activate the sense receptors in our neurology. From there our eyes, ears, skin, etc. transform and transduce this "information" from those forms to neuro-electrical forms as the "information" moves from neuron to neuron to the brain where it becomes transformed into bio-chemical forms. There we have the impression of "sights, sounds, sensations, smells, tastes, balance, etc." Yet this phenomenological impression of the interaction of our eyes, ears, and skin with the world only exists as a facsimile or representation of the world—not the world itself, nor the actual cortical "mapping."

Truly, we do not operate on the world directly—but indirectly, via our maps and maps of maps.

What significance does this play in our experiences? All the difference in the world. In the NLP model, Bandler and Grinder, and then Robert Dilts along with others, identified more specifically how our *neurological maps* and *linguistic maps* interplay to create the structure of our subjective experiences. The highlights of their discoveries include the following:

- Most people have and use a *favorite representational system (RS)* as they represent and code information.

- We have both *lead input channels* and *representational channels* in our processing of information and map-making and oftentimes these differ.

- When we input information using one language system and code it in another, this generates "fuzzy functions." This refers to cross-over circuits so that we might see-feel (V-K), or feel-hear (K-A), or hear-see (A-V), etc. Such "synesthesias" may work to enhance or impoverish our experiences.

- We can so under-use a RS that we receive very little input from that channel (e. g. few images, sounds, sensations). This will typically impoverish our maps, and we will lack critical information about such distinctions.

- Sometimes when we input in one system and code in another, we can seemingly have no awareness of the sights, sounds, sensations, etc. of the input.

- Any of the language systems can operate in a "meta" position to any other. This makes **all** of the information from all of the systems *para-messages* and means that none exist as more "real" or important than any other. Yet, if we use a system to *comment on* another system, it becomes a meta-message. A sigh can comment on a statement and then another statement can comment on the sigh.

- Learning to be aware of someone's favorite RS provides a way to "speak that persons' language." Doing this hastens and increases the sense of connectedness and rapport. By so *pacing* a person we build a bridge for "trust."

- Much misunderstanding and miscommunication results from a war of the RS. People simply use different input and output channels and so do not connect with each other. They don't match or pace each other's VAK systems.

- Switching RS not only gives us the ability to speak another's language, but to enrich both person's models of the world.

- Mapping over from one RS to another enriches our maps with the result that we have more choices and more skills.

- When we use an inappropriate RS in a particular area or skill, it creates problems, difficulties, and limitations. Learning to match RS to skills and re-mapping (re-coding) according to the RS appropriateness can suddenly make skills and abilities possible (e. g. using the visual system for spelling, the auditory-tonal channel for music appreciation and skill, the kinesthetic language system for archery, etc.).

- When we identify inappropriate synesthesias, we can then break them up and use the sensory language systems more appropriately (e. g. a nurse see-seeing blood rather than see-feeling; hear-hearing tones and volumes rather than hear-feeling).

All of these insights and procedures arise from the simple (yet so profound) understanding of **the map-territory distinction**. If Korzybski's aphorism, *"the map is not the territory,"* holds true for words, it also holds true for the sensory representations. Yet this neurological language system of the representational systems exists at a deeper level of abstraction than does language. Language exists *above* the primary level of the VAK representational system and so inherently functions as a meta-level system. For this reason, we may feel more tempted to "believe in our senses" than we might "believe in our words." Yet both only exist as constructions, as representations, as symbols. Neither "are" real. Both sensory-based representations and linguistic based representations arise as constructions and abstractions of our nervous system.

> *"The statement by Korzybski that 'the map is not the territory' is true in two major ways. First, we, as humans, create models of our world which we use as a guide for our behavior. Second, we have a number of different maps available to represent our experiences—kinesthetic, visual, auditory, natural language, etc. These maps of our experience do not necessarily represent only information from the direct input channels of the senses to associated representational systems."* (1976, p. 25)

Now we have many different **languages** to meta-model and to enrich and, as we do, we have many channels by which to do "magical" things. Sometimes a whole new world suddenly comes into existence by simply adding an under-used representational system. Sometimes a new strategy and skills arises from learning to use the most appropriate RS. Sometimes lapping over from one to another empowers us in new and exciting ways.

When Maps Multiply

When we add the neurological maps of the representational systems to the meta-representation system of words we discover that each of us has a multiple number of language systems by which to input, process, and code the territory. Further, given the varying strengths and weaknesses of our sensory systems, how we favor some systems over others, etc., it makes sense that we may end up having different models of the world in the different systems.

What sign indicates that we have conflicting maps of the world jarring and warring inside of us? **Incongruity.** The messages carried by the various output channels may not fit together or coalesce as a single meaning. The guiding paradigms of our lives may themselves jar and jolt against each other. Recognizing that all such messages from our various sensory channels exist as **para-messages**, Bandler and Grinder (1976) took issue with Bateson on that point. They developed their model based upon the assumption that,

> *"...we accept each message as an equally valid representation of that person's experience. In our model, no one of these paramessages can be said to be more valid—or truer, or more representative of the client—than any other. No one of a set of paramessages can be said to be meta to any other member of its set. Rather, our understanding of a set of paramessages is that each of these messages represents a portion of the client's model of the world. When the client is communicating congruently, each of the paramessages matches, fits with, is congruent with each of the others. This tells us that all of the models which the client is using to guide his behavior at that point in time are consistent ... When the client is communicating incongruently, we know that the models of the world which he is using to guide his behavior are inconsistent."* (p. 38)

No message inherently operates in a meta relationship to another. And yet we can use any message or representational system to make a comment on another. That which makes a message **meta to** another arises from *our use of it,* namely, when we use it to make a message **about** the other message. Thus a word or sentence that *comments on* a gesture, facial expression, pointing of a finger, tone of voice, etc., then operates meta to those non-verbal messages. And if we point our finger in reference to a word, as a comment on that word, then the finger gesture plays a meta-role to the word in that particular sequence of events. For us to label a message (A) *meta to* another message (B), then "A is a message about B (equivalently, A has B in its scope—the Bateson/Russell condition)." (1976, p. 41).

To effectively respond to the meta-experience of conflicting maps which shows up emotionally and behaviorally as incongruity, Bandler and Grinder suggested that we first identify and sort the incongruencies, and then integrate them. Identifying such necessitates that we develop greater sensory acuity to the visual, auditory, and kinesthetic channels, listen for such linguistic cues as "but," or "an implied but" that expresses a statement with a slight rise in intonation at the end of the sentence (pp. 55-57). Another indicator occurs when the right and left sides of a person's body look (or operate) out of sync (p. 58).

Integrating such involves "going meta" (taking a meta-position) and meta-commenting or meta-questioning."How do you feel *about* feeling angry?" By assisting a person to achieve a meta-position to his or her own polarities, then one can make contact between the polarities in the same system. This leads to the "magic" that people find in playing polarities, a Satir "parts party," psychodrama, enactment techniques, etc. Out of this came the "magic" of the Visual Squash Pattern (pp. 86-88) whereby we can generate a new neuro-linguistic integration.

When Maps Intersect

Multiple maps do not always conflict. Sometimes they merge and interface in a smooth way so that they create more power—*the power of congruency.* Yet generally, the more maps we have, the more possibilities arise for potential conflicts. These multiple mappings also invite maps to *intersect* in such a way that we switch from one to the other without awareness of so doing. A person who speaks two or more languages may frequently experience this phenomenon of switching from English to German or Russian or Hebrew or whatever. This *cross-over circuit*—going from one map suddenly to another often beautifully enriches description, choices, and skills.

Years of backpacking the high country in Colorado have taught me the advantage of using several kinds of maps—highway road maps to get to a location, then shifting to a topographical map to navigate the mountains, to using Forest Rangers' maps to find camping areas, restrooms, etc.

A similar operation occurs when we bring information in via the visual system, encode it kinesthetically, and output it linguistically. Such **synesthesias** serve as the neurological foundations for the semantic ill-formedness that shows up in Cause-Effect and Mind-Reading statements as well as Complex Equivalences. Thus:

"You make me angry."

This semantically ill-formed sentence may have arisen from someone seeing or hearing a stimulus that they disliked (e. g., a tone, facial gesture, etc.). To that stimulus, they automatically and unconsciously evaluate it in a negative way. They see-feel or hear-feel. The *cross-over wiring* (synesthesia) from seeing (V) to feeling (K) occurs so quickly, automatically, and unconsciously, that it comes out in language as "You causative verb X feel this emotion." Yet in assigning the cause of this cause-effect relationship to something outside the person's nervous system, and therefore outside his or her control, we thereby create and express an ill-formedness in structure.

Synesthesias serve as the neurological foundations of Mind-Reading, Cause-Effect, and Complex Equivalences. Here, rather than making distinctions, we let our sensations merge. As we hear tones—we see different colors. As we see different numbers—we hear different tones. As we see a beautiful painting—we feel different internal kinesthetic sensations. Child psychologists have noted the lack of differentiation in infants and young children—that differentiating between themselves and stimuli that strike the sense organs involves a learning process. They have noted also that we all tend to first represent stimuli (noise, sights, etc.) as kinesthetic sensations.

> "In traditional psychophysics, this term, fuzzy function, is most closely translated by the term synesthesia. ... fuzzy functions are not bad, crazy or evil, and the outcome of what we consider effective therapy is not the elimination of these functions, but rather the realization that these functions can be the basis for much creative activity..." (p. 101)

In Mind-Reading, we typically activate feel-see or feel-hear circuits. Here we begin with a feeling of some sort and then use sights and sounds to project the feelings upon.

> "... in the case of Mind Reading ... the client takes body sensations—his kinesthetic representation—and distorts the information arriving visually and auditorially from outside him in such a way that it conforms to his body sensations." (p. 102)

Thus, "When you look at me that way (use that tone of voice) I know that you dislike me and think I'm worthless."

In Cause-Effect statements, we see-hear, see-feel, hear-feel, etc. Here we see or hear or even feel a stimulus and selectively focus on it in such a way as to think (map out) that that stimulus actually *causes (makes, forces)* us to experience certain feelings, or other responses. Thus, "You make me so depressed when you talk in that tone." "You make me sick with your negativity." "You make me angry slurping like that."

We can even identify **merged, intersected maps** by listening to the unique arrangement of predicates that they produce.

> You look so warm in that outfit.
> The judge appeared to me to be a really cold man.
> From what you've said, I can't see how to get a hold
> of this concept.
> Clearly, this experience has been hard on you.
> I feel your despair. It rings clear as a bell to me.

Both impoverishing and empowering "magic" can arise from synesthesias—our cross-circuit maps. Bandler and Grinder postulated that asthma results from see-feel and hear-feel representations of another's aggression toward them—storing such in their bodies (especially their neck and throat). They suggested that sadism involves see-feel circuits in which visual input of another's pain gets represented as kinesthetic pleasure (p. 117). Violence results from visual input represented kinesthetically (see-feel) so that seeing a dis-value in another person for whom we feel responsible may activate the motor responses (pp. 107-109).

Multiple Intersecting (Or Conflicting) Maps In A Human System

So we begin with a single "system" of an single individual. Here we have multiple levels of models of the world which can intersect in multiple ways as visual map interfaces with auditory map which interfaces with kinesthetic map which interfaces with the linguistic map which interfaces with the visual map, etc. Given that, how much more can multiple maps explode into even more levels of complexity when we consider several other people coming into this context—each with multiple maps?

This introduces the part that *Family Systems* (from Virginia Satir) played in the initial NLP model. Bandler and Grinder, having modeled Virginia and therefore *Family Systems Therapy* in *The Structure of Magic II* offered descriptions of shared **maps** operating as a *system.* They opened up the frame for considering what happens when two or more people interact and become a system (a family, a couple, a business, company, group).

> *"To accept the family as the system unit for therapy is to use an overall strategy to work with the family as if it were one living organism, each member being an essential part and resource..."* (1976, p. 126)

The *system* of a family, in fact, operates not only as "one living organism" itself, but also provides one of the most important **contexts** to which we adapt ourselves and learn the patterns that we do. Thus we meta-model the individuals in any given system to discover their maps and "the system" as a whole—the "rules" and generalizations that we have developed inside a system for coping and interacting. Meta-modeling "the system" means learning to see what **emerges** from all of the interacting patterns in terms of family beliefs, rules, processes, etc. And central to this lies the meta-model distinction of Cause-Effect.

> *"In our experience, in every family or couple we have encountered, we have identified the particular form of semantic-illformedness called Cause-Effect semantic ill-formedness—the situation in which one member of the family is represented as causing another family member to experience some feeling or emotion."* (1976, p. 128)

The "magic" of transformation begins by meta-modeling the specific representations of *present state and desired state* of each person. Next comes exploring how the individual maps intersect with each other, where the system itself prevents accessing the needed resources, and opening up more channels so that the system can accept and use feedback to evolve itself. By meta-modeling the parts of the system (e. g. what each member wants, how each member currently views the situation, what resources each needs, etc.), a consultant can hear and see the current maps of the members, the system's maps, and then explore what prevents them from fully experiencing their desired maps.

Groups, businesses, and families typically get into pain due to the impoverished maps (and impoverishing maps) that they use to navigate the world. These usually involve maps that prevent the members from openly and flexibly receiving current feedback. A system with rules against seeing, hearing, feeling, and speaking to each other, and/or a system that has become calibrated to each other so that now they only react already assuming that they know what the other means, has become a closed and rigid system.

Conclusion

The "magic" for changing our neuro-linguistic and neuro-semantic reality does not depend upon words only. We have more *"language" systems* within our repertoire for creating representations or maps than just words. We have several sensory-based representational systems—the visual, auditory, kinesthetic, olfactory, and gustatory systems.

We do not move through life with just *one* model of the world— we have numerous models, numerous models at various logical levels, and numerous models that we have awarenesses of consciously and those that run various programs apart from conscious awareness. As a result, we can easily become torn, conflicted, and at odds with ourselves, thereby reducing our personal power, congruency, and integrity. Such internal map wars generate various "parts" or facets of ourselves which then try to navigate by one map while other "parts" attempt to do so by other models. No wonder we feel torn in different directions at times.

Then two of these different mapping processes can merge in such a way that we input in one system and then process using another map. The cross-circuit synesthesias that result from such mapping overlaps can create some of the highest expressions of creativity, genius, and power in human functioning. It can also create some of our most tormenting demons. Again, the magic goes back to the mapping and to the structure that we have built and organized in our models of the world.

When we put together one human being with so many multiple mapping processes at so many logical levels with another human being who experiences the same kind of complexity—the interactive communicational and relational systems that result can sometimes seem overwhelming to those of us who typically operate only with $7^{+/-2}$ chunks of information at a time! And yet, the magical kind of things we can do inter-personally as we communicate and relate has structure. And the structure of that magic simply builds upon the foundational principles of how we language ourselves and others in the first place.

Epilogue

And The Magic Continues ...

In several recent trainings on *Conversational Magic*, I have spoken the following as a benediction to conclude the workshops. So I use it here as a benediction to this work. It serves as an update to John and Richard's original statement in **The Structure of Magic** (1975).

> *"Magic is hidden in the language we speak. The webs that you can tie and untie are at your command if only you pay attention to what you already have (language) and the structure of the incantations for growth..."* (p. 19)

Magic lies hidden in the language we speak.
In a process world of ongoing and ever-changing Events
nothing inherently means anything,
And yet, magically, everything can mean something.
Because with words and symbols at your command,
you can cast spells as you weave together a web of words.
And so you link Internal States with Events in the world
to thereby call forth *neuro-linguistic magic*.
Then for good measure you wrap your spell
with higher level contexts and frames,
meanings within meanings,
and those meanings embedded in yet higher meanings.
The spells you cast then lie at your command
if only you pay attention
to your magic wand of Symbolism
and its Secrets about the Structure of Magic.

A long time ago Sigmund Freud (1915-1917) noted that *"Words were originally magic,"* and to this day words have retained much of their ancient magical power." (p. 17, italics added). He noted how that by words we can "make" each other blissfully happy and/or can "drive" each other into the depths of despair. He made these notations about *words* in the context of therapy having noted that nothing happens in treatment "but an exchange of words."

Today we extend our definition of *"language"* itself to include gestures, facial expressions, tones, pitches, volumes, silences, and all of the other things that we do in signaling and cuing ourselves and others. *Language,* as involving numerous symbol systems, includes much more than just words. It includes non-verbal expressions and multiple non-propositional language forms.

This book, as an update and re-visit to **the model of word "magic,"** grew out of the original genius that John and Richard created. In that work, they bequeathed us numerous keys for beginning to understand *the structure of magic* and to use *the secrets of neuro-linguistic magic.* Thus their Meta-model originally enlightened us about the inner structure of magic by pointing us in the direction of how to tap into it and how to use it for enhancing our lives. Now with this extension of *magic's structure* and many of **the secrets** that drive the magic—we can go further and begin to build even more *incantations of growth, excellence, and even genius.* Magic does get to evolve!

So **magic** indeed lies hidden in the language that we speak. It lies in the self-languaging that we engage in as we think, dream, imagine, rehearse, question, etc. It lies in how we language our descriptions of the world, how we language difficulties and problems, and even in how we language our relationships. It lies in how we language others. By such languaging, we weave our incantational webs.

May you now *take command* of your languaging as you utter numerous incantations for yourself and others today. May you find yourself *paying attention* in new and useful ways to the "magic" of your words so that you begin to feel yourself tuning up your linguistic ears to *the music of the magic* all around you! May you become a *neuro-linguistic magician* so that you become a blessing to all those who you touch—and thereby significantly enrich our world!

Michael Hall

Appendix

Appendix

Appendix A

Meta-Model Changes

I have made several changes in this updating and expanding of the Meta-model. The following identifies some of these and offers some explanations:

1. From Therapy Specific to General Language Use. In their original work, Richard Bandler and John Grinder presented their findings about language initially in the context of "therapy." Later they discovered that "the Meta-model of language **in therapy**" also applied to all other forms of human language use in business, education, sports, medicine, etc. Thereafter they, and NLP, dropped the last two words, "in therapy."

Throughout the text of this updating I have sought consistently to drop the psychotherapeutic context. Of course, I did not change the *content* when I made quotations from *The Structure of Magic*. So in those quotes you will still find the predominance of the psychotherapy content, hence such terms as "clients," "therapy," "in therapy," etc. In the text proper, I have dropped the use of "client" and "therapy," and have simply used "person."

The phrase "in therapy" (e. g. "The client's response fails to be well formed in therapy") refers to languaging "for healing" from emotional distress, or "for becoming whole." In this model of human functioning, this involves languaging a person in such a way that he or she can begin to operate in the world with enriched maps rather than impoverished ones.

2. From Dependence Upon the "Aspects" Model of Noam Chomsky. In the original development of the Meta-model, Bandler and Grinder depended heavily upon Chomsky's **Transformational Grammar** (TG) model. And yet, about the same time that they published the Meta-model, TG in its original form had already become outdated as its adherents showed the model inadequate as an explanatory model in the field of Linguistics. Gross (1979) attempted to construct a transformational generative grammar of French, but failed. He noted that the project became "much more complex than expected" and ultimately turned out "to be entirely taxonomic. This result calls into question the validity of the so-called theory of generative grammar." (p. 859).

In the years that have passed, the *Aspects* model (1956) that Chomsky developed and championed have continued to undergo changes and developments. Harris (1993) charted much of this change in his book, ***The Linguistic Wars***. There he detailed the in-house conflicts that arose between Chomsky and his students many years prior to 1975. Before the publication of ***The Structure of Magic***, in fact, *Generative Semantics* had split off from Chomsky's model under the visionary leadership of Lakoff, McCawley, Ross, and others. Bandler and Grinder wrote one brief note in ***The Structure of Magic*** about *Generative Semantics* (See Note #6 after Chapter Four, p. 109).

Generative Semantics took the idea of deep structure (DS), that eventually led them to the domain of "meaning" (semantics) and ran with it. They ran with it much further than Chomsky could personally endure. As a result, Chomsky backed away from his deep structure hypothesis and began to posit that transformations occurred also at the surface structures (SS). First, Chomsky renamed it "D-structure" and later dispensed with it entirely.

Eventually, Transformational Grammar gave way to new linguistic models—Chomsky's Generative Grammar and then EST (Extended Standard Theory) and to Lakoff's Generative Semantics. Yet these models also could not provide a completely satisfactory description or explanation of linguistic phenomena. During the 1980s and 1990s ever newer models continued to arise.

A great many of the former linguists of the TG school have followed Lakoff and others into cognitive grammar. Langacker produced two massive two-volume ***Foundations of Cognitive Grammar*** (1987/ 1991), and ***Concept, Image, and Symbol*** (1991) which seem to come closer and closer to the representational model of NLP.

The original *"Aspects"* of Chomsky has, in the passing years, become more and more dated as an adequate model as various cognitive linguistics have taken its place. Chomsky and colleagues helped to bring this about as they pushed the transformational grammar model and thereby increasingly discovered more and more irregularities and inadequacies to that paradigm. These inadequacies of transformational grammar, and especially "deep structure" to explain language, eventually undermined it.

What does this do to the Meta-model? To what extend does the Meta-model depend upon transformational grammar? Does the exposure of inadequacy in transformational grammar undermine the Meta-model?

As I have examined and re-examined the Meta-model in *The Structure of Magic*, Bandler and Grinder clearly *began* within the context of the transformational grammar and certainly grounded much of their model upon its formulations. Without doubt, they depended upon, and used, *the terminology* which they received from transformational grammar. They also depended upon the general distinction between the DS and SS which played such a crucial role in Chomsky's model in the 1960s and 1970s.

And yet, while admitting that much reliance, overall *the Meta-model does **not** depend upon transformational grammar* at all. After all, Transformational Grammar (TG) addresses an entirely different question, and therefore a very different domain, from that which NLP or the Meta-model (MM) addresses. As a linguistic theory TG, (as does any Linguistic Model), sought to provide an explanatory model and the necessary and sufficient mechanisms for the syntactical structure of language, language acquisition, the relation between sound and meaning, phonology, morphology, etc.

NLP, and especially the Meta-model, does **not** address or speak to this domain at all. It therefore does not exist or operate as *a linguistic model* at all. After all, we do **not** use it to describe or explain linguistic phenomena. Our focus lies **not** in theorizing about the interrelationships between grammar, symbolism, syntax, or meaning. We rather use it as a *neuro-linguistic* model. We use it to explain the *effect* of language in human neurology, experience, and inner "reality."

How the transformations occur, or what transformational rules sufficiently explain the processes, do not concern the functioning of the Meta-model (MM) at all. Typically, most NLP-ers know very little about the transformational rules or functioning. Such has nothing to do with using the model—and it plays no role whatever in understanding the NLP understanding of the *structure of magic* that occurs in human neurology.

Rather than delving to the depths required in a linguistic theory about the cognitive mechanisms that govern language, the Meta-model focuses on *the phenomenological level of nervous system* and upon psychological abstracting. So although Bandler and Grinder devoted a lot of attention to TG, and even provided an introductory appendix about TG (Appendix A, p. 183), the model actually does **not** depend on it at all.

The Meta-model actually correlates much more to the *General-Semantics* of Alfred Korzybski than to TG. Korzybski, who originally coined the term *neuro-linguistics*, cared much more about the *neurological semantics* (hence his term *neuro-semantics)* than he did about linguistic mechanisms. He described General Semantics as "a new extensional discipline which explains and trains us how to use our nervous systems most efficiently" (1933: p. xxvi)—how to actually "run your own brain."

The Meta-model obviously begins with a person's *surface expressions* which formulate understandings and representations. Here we encounter a person's most conscious expression of one's cognitive maps. The Meta-model then assumes and posits that below, behind, or above (depending upon your metaphor of choice) we inevitably have a richer and fuller phenomenological map. Here the terminology of *deep structure and surface structure* served them with well and provided them a basic logical level format of human mapping. We see a similar concept in Cognitive Grammar in that *above* any word or term we have various cognitive domains (categories) and then matrixes of categories—contexts and contexts-of-contexts that set the frame and which govern meaning.

Bandler and Grinder then adopted the cognitive presupposition that people operate via some kind of cognitive map of the world, others, and themselves. Yet because the human nervous system always and inevitably "leaves characteristics out" (Korzybski), "deletes" significant information (Bandler and Grinder), and functions as a "reducing valve" (Huxley), *the process of inquiring* about that cognitive map helps the person to expand and enrich it. Yet this formulation does not depend upon TG. It reflects a basic cognitive or constructivist frame. It suggests that by facilitating someone to "go back inside" to their earlier reference maps, we can enable them to re-map so that they have a more accurate and useful map to operate from. This then updates the limiting and impoverishing parts as well as corrects erroneous facets.

The bottom line? The meta-model depends only upon *the phenomenological constructivism* implied (and supplied) by TG. We can just as adequately build the meta-model upon the abstracting model of Korzybski. We can do that because the Meta-model only posits that consciousness operates at various **levels of abstracting** (1975: pp. 158-159).

The General Semantics epistemological model that Korzybski developed actually provides a much fuller and more accurate paradigm for the Meta-model. After all, it first and foremost relates to **neurology**—to how our nervous system (which includes our brain and physiology) *abstracts* from the world of energy manifestations and makes various *transforms* along the way as it codes and recodes the "information" in the nervous system. Korzybski's *structural differential* model designates levels and orders from various deeper structures to increasingly higher structures. This keeps the general format of the "deep structure" of neuro-linguistic and neuro-semantic representation and higher structures without needing to bring over wholesale everything in the transformational grammar model.

Further, this emphasis on human "abstracting" (abstractions) fits very well into the more recent work of Lakoff (1987) who puts similar emphasis on human "cognition" as:

- **Embodied.** Our conceptual systems grow out of bodily experience and make sense in terms of such. "The core of our conceptual systems is directly grounded in perception, body movement, and experience of a physical and social character" (p. xiv). This embodiment of "thought" means that thought and reason does not exist as "the mechanical manipulation of abstract symbols."

- **Imaginative.** Cognitive concepts go beyond literal mirroring or representations of external reality and partake of imaginative features involving metaphors, metonymies, and images based on experience and bodily experience. Langacker (1991) goes even further, describing "grammar as image." In his works, he focuses on the dimensions of imagery using figure/ground, profile/base, scanning operations, etc.

- **Gestalt properties.** Rather than being "atomistic," concepts take on systemic features—features which *emerge* to create an overall configuration that exists as so much more than the sum of the parts.

- **Experientialism.** Lakoff labels this "experiential realism" and defines it as saying that yes, there is a real world out there—a reality that places constraints on us, but that what we experience as "real" depends also in part upon how we conceive, conceptualize, and construct that reality.

- **Categorizing.** Lakoff has popularized the work of Eleanor Rosch who developed *prototype theory* of categories. Langacker has brought much of this work into *Cognitive Grammar* and used it to construct new formulations for the "categorizing relationships" that explain language. Prototype theory differs significantly from the classical Aristotelian presentation of categories.

Linguistics Vs. *Neuro*-Linguistics

While Grinder and Bandler originally founded NLP's Meta-model upon formulations from the field of linguistics, their models do **not** function as *linguistic* models in the same sense. Their goals and purposes differ radically from those of formal and theoretical linguistics. Various linguistic models, from Transformational Grammar, Generative Semantics, Space Grammar, to Cognitive Grammar seek primarily to understand and identify *theoretically* how language works. Such endeavors aims to model the processes of language, linguistic phenomena, language acquisition, etc. As such, they offer no evaluation about the value or usefulness of nominalizations, universals, modals, tree structures, derivations, etc. in human functioning.

By way of contrast, the General Semantics and NLP models (i. e. the Structural Differential, the Meta-model) do *not* address such linguistic concerns. Rather they focus on *neuro*-linguistic *experience* in the *psycho-logical* (Korzybski's terminology) life of the human being. Korzybski especially emphasized that while the older "semantics" focused primarily on theories of *verbal* meanings, his "general semantics" did not. He rather sought to deal only with *neuro*-semantic and *neuro*-linguistic living reactions of individuals.

Similarly with the Meta-model—it focuses primarily on identifying poor mapping (ill-formedness) that prevents full living. In this it transcends grammar and grammatical, syntactical, morphological, etc. problems and issues. Our *neuro-linguistic model* seeks only to identify expressions that mark out problem areas in mapping (in one's schema or model of the world) that effect psychological functioning (how we think, feel, speak, behave, relate, etc.). We use this model to identity and address the cognitive mapping distortions that generate human difficulties. And we do so in order to assist people in developing more enhancing phenomenological models of the world. So the "linguistic distinctions" of the Meta-model operate as markers of places where we might find neuro-linguistic mapping problems. Then, by offering the "challenges," it seeks to perform its **transformational magic.**

Cognitive Grammar

In studying the latest developments in Cognitive Grammar, I have found that these newer developments in Linguistics seem to provide a theoretical system that continue to support the NLP Meta-model.

In fact, in some ways it provides even better and more thorough support. Langacker (1991), for instance,has completely rejected and moved on from the Chomsky transformational grammar model. Instead he has equated *meaning with conceptualization* and has built a system of linguistic semantics based upon providing structural analysis and explicit description of abstract entities like "thoughts" and "concepts." Accordingly, this sends him to *cognitive processing itself.*

> *"Because conceptualization resides in cognitive processing, our ultimate objective must be to characterize the types of cognitive events whose occurrence constitutes a given mental experience."*
> (p. 2)

Langacker broadly interprets "conceptualization." For him, it encompasses "novel conceptions as well as fixed concepts; sensory, kinesthetic, and emotive experience." Thus he begins with the sensory-based level of representation. He also includes recognition of "contexts" (social, physical, linguistic, etc.). This brings in the abstract representations at higher logical levels. He then adds other qualifications: *entrenchment* to refer to the habitual and solidified concepts that have become fixed in a community, *cognitive salience* to refer to differing degrees of importance, *semantic structures* or domains that a conceptualizer uses, *extensions and elaborations* to refer to new and novel uses of concepts, and *network* to identify that we experience thoughts within matrixes and hierarchies of concepts.

In doing this, Cognitive Grammar utilizes the new work of Rosch and Lakoff in distinguishing traditional categories from prototype category theory. This enables us to "think" in degrees of prototype and use a highest-level schema or a schema that does not fit the prototype. Thinking utilizes various cognitive domains in order to "make sense of" something as it creates meaning. Such domains can refer to any sort of conceptualization: a perceptual experience, a concept, a conceptual complex, an elaborate knowledge system, etc. As we use such domains, we thereby generate various "cognitive routines" for ourselves and by these we construct our models of the world.

These newer Cognitive linguistic models highlight the *representational value* of concepts in a way that the old transformational grammar did not. In these models, our grammatical expressions reflect our cognitive processing—the entities and processes that we imagine and symbolize, how we profile figures up against various backgrounds, what stands out saliently for us, the trajectors in our language that move through this "grammar space" to various landmarks, etc.

They also provide a construct of logical levels as they posit hierarchies of conceptual complexity. We used to use "deep structure" to conceptually posit an underlying level of neuro-linguistic mapping. Now the new cognitive grammars posit cognitive domains and network of domains arranged in hierarchies. A person goes to these over-arching contexts (domains) to "get" their fuller model of the world that only shows up in abbreviated form in their everyday expressions.

Appendix B

There Is No "Is"

Question: To what extent did you even notice that I wrote this book using the device of **E-Prime** (except for quotes from others)? As noted earlier under **Identifications** (#7 in Chapter 4), this refers to **English**-*primed* of the "to be" verb family of passive verbs (is, am, are, was, were, be, being, been). Invented by D. David Bourland, Jr. and popularized by Bourland and Paul Dennithorne Johnston in *To Be or Not: An E-Prime Anthology*, E-Prime and E-Choice empowers people to not fall into the "is" traps of language.

The "is" traps? Yes, Alfred Korzybski (1941/1994) warned that *the "is" of identity* and *the "is" of predication* present two dangerous linguistic and semantic constructions that map false-to-fact conclusions. The first has to do with identity—how we identify a thing or what we identify ourselves with, and the second with attribution, how we frequently project our "stuff" onto others or onto things without realizing it.

Identity as "sameness in all respects," does not even exist. It can't. At the sub-microscopic level, everything involves a "dance of electrons" always moving, changing, and becoming. So no thing can ever "stay the same" even with itself. So nothing "is" in any static, permanent, unchanging way. Since nothing exists as eternal, but since everything continually changes, then nothing "is." To use "is" mis-speaks, mis-evaluates, and mis-maps reality. To say, "She is lazy..." "That is a stupid statement..." falsely maps reality. And Korzybski argued that unsanity and insanity ultimately lies in *identifications.*

Predication refers to "asserting" something. So to say, "This is good," "That flower is red," "He is really stupid!" creates a language structure which implies that something "out there" contains these qualities of "goodness," "redness," and "stupidity." The "is" suggests that such things exist *independent of the speaker's experience.* Not so. Our descriptions speak primarily about our internal experience indicating our judgments and values. More accurately we could have said, "I evaluate as good this or that," "I see that flower as red," "I think of him as suffering from stupidity!"

"Is" statements falsely distract, confuse logical levels, and subtly lead us to think that such value judgments exist outside our skin in the world "objectively." Wrong again. The evaluations (good, red, stupid) function as definitions and interpretations in the speaker's mind.

The "to be" verbs dangerously presuppose that "things" (actually events or processes) stay the same. Not! These verbs invite us to create mental representations of fixedness so that we begin to set the world in concrete and to live in "a frozen universe." These verbs code the dynamic nature of processes statically. "Life is tough." "I am no good at math."

Do these statements not sound definitive? Absolute? "That's just the way it is!" No wonder Bourland calls "is" "am" and "are," etc. *"the deity mode."* "The fact is that this work is no good!" Such words carry a sense of completeness, finality, and time-independence. Yet discerning the difference between the map and the territory tells us these phenomena exist on different logical levels. Using E-Prime (or E-Choice) reduces slipping in groundless authoritarian statements which only closes minds or invites arguments.

If we confuse the language we use in describing reality (our map) with reality (the territory), then we *identify* differing things. And that makes for unsanity. **There "is" no is.** "Is" non-references. It points to nothing in reality. It operates entirely as an irrational construction of the human mind. Its use leads to semantic mis-evaluations.

Conversely, writing, thinking, and speaking in E-Prime contributes to *"consciousness of abstracting"* (conscious awareness) that we make maps of the world which inherently differ from the world. E-Prime enables us to think and speak with more clarity and precision as it forces us to take first-person. This reduces the passive verb tense ("It was done." "Mistakes were made."). It

restores speakers to statements, thereby contextualizing statements. E-Prime, by raising consciousness of abstracting, thereby
enables us to index language. Now I realize that the person I met
last week, Person$_{last week}$, "is" not equal in all respects to the person
who now stands before me, Person$_{this week}$. This assist me in making
critical and valuable distinctions.

E-Choice differs from E-Prime. It does not take such a radical
view. Thus, it allows one to use *the "is" of existence* (e. g. "Where is
your office?" "It is on 7th Street at Orchard Avenue."), *the auxiliary "is"* (e. g. "He is coming next week.") and *the "is" of name,*
(e.g. "What is your name?" "It is Michael." "My name is Bob.").

Appendix C

The Meta-Levels Of The Meta-Model

————Structure————
Metaphor (Met)
Presuppositions (Ps)
Multiordinality (M)
Identification (Id)

————Distortion————
Mind-Reading (MR)
Complex Equivalences (CEq)
Nominalizations (Nom)
Cause-Effect (C-E)
Lost Performatives (LP)
Delusional Verbal Splits (DVS)
Pseudo-Words (PW)
Personalizing (Per)
Static Words (SW)

————Generalization————
Universal Quantifiers (UQ)
Model Operators (MO)
Either-Or Phrases (E-O)
Over/Under Defined Terms (O/U)

Evaluative Based Language
——-Deletion——-
Deletions — Simple (Del)
Deletions—Comparative/ Superlative
(Unspecified Relations) (UR)
Unspecified Referential Indices
(Unspecified Nouns & Verbs) (URI)
Unspecified Processes —
Adverbs Modifying Verbs (UP-Adv)
Unspecified Processes —
Adjectives Modifying Nouns (UP-
Adj)

Challenging the Assumptive Structure
• The Assumptive Formats or Frames
• Map-Territory Confusions

Challenging Distortions
• Specifying the knowledge source
• Specifying logical level confusions
• Specifying equations
• Specifying causations, syntax, order
• Specifying referents
• Hyphenating

Challenging Generalizations
• Challenging the Allness
• Challenging the Rules
• Challenging the One-Valued Structure
• Challenging the Two-Valued Structure
• Challenging the specificity

Indexing Deleted References
• Specifying the what, when, who, where, how, etc.
• Representationally Tracking referents

Sensory-Based Language
Descriptive

Person A in communication

Sensory-Based Language

with Person B

Appendix D

The New And Updated Meta-Model

Patterns/ Distinctions	Responses/ Challenges	Predictions/ Results
1. Simple Deletions		
"They don't listen to me."	Who specifically doesn't listen to you?	Recover the Deletion
"People push me around."	Who specifically pushes you	Recover the Ref. Index
2. Comparative and Superlative Deletions **(Unspecified Relations)**		
"She's a better person."	Better than whom? Better at what? Compared to whom, what? Given what criteria?	Recover the deleted standard, criteria, or belief
3. Unspecified Referential Indices **(Unspecified Nouns and Verbs)**		
"I am uncomfortable."	Uncomfortable in what way? Uncomfortable when?	Recover specific qualities of the verb
"They don't listen to me."	Who specifically doesn't listen to you?	Recover the nouns of
"He said that she was mean."	Who specifically said that? Whom did he say that you call mean? What did he mean by 'mean'?	the persons involved Recover the individual meaning of the term
"People push me around."	Who specifically pushes you?	Add details to the map
"I felt really manipulated."	Manipulated in what way and how?	
4. Unspecified Processes—Adverbs Modifying Verbs		
"Surprisingly, my father lied about his drinking."	How did you feel surprised about that? What surprised you about that?	Recovers the process of the person's emotional state
"She slowly started to cry."	What indicated to you that her starting to cry occurred in a slow manner?	Enriches with details the person's referent
5. Unspecified Processes—Adjectives Modifying Nouns		
"I don't like unclear people."	Unclear about what and in what way?	Recovers the speaker's
"The unhappy letter surprised me."	How, and in what way, did you feel unhappy about the letter?	projected sense of feeling "unclear" or "unhappy."
6. Universal Quantifiers		
"She never listens to me."	Never? She has never so much as listened to you even a little bit?	Recovers details about the extent of a process and counter-examples.

7. Modal Operators
(Operational Modes of Being)

"I have to take care of her."	What would happen if you did?	Recovers details of the
"I can't tell him the truth."	What wouldn't happen if you didn't?	process, also causes,
	"You have to or else what?"	effects, and outcomes.

8. Lost Performatives
(Evaluative statement(s) with the speaker deleted or unowned)

"It's bad to be inconsistent."	Who evaluates it as bad?	Recovers the source of
	According to what standard?	idea or belief—the
	How do you determine this label	map-maker, standards
	used, of "badness?" etc.	

9. Nominalizations
(Pseudo-Nouns that hide processes and actions)

"Let's improve our communication."	Whose communicating do you mean?	Recovers the process
	How would you like to communicate?	and the characteristics left out
"What state did you wake up in this morning?"	How specifically did you feel, think, etc.?	Specifies the verb and actions
	What behaviors, physiology, and internal representations make up this "state?"	

10. Mind-Reading
(Attributing knowledge of another's internal thoughts, feelings, motives)

"You don't like me..."	How do you know I don't like you?	Recovers the source of
	What evidence leads you to that	the information—
	how a person knows	specifies conclusion?

11. Cause-Effect
(Causational statements of relations between events, stimulus-response beliefs)

"You make me sad."	How does my behavior cause you	Recovers understanding
	to respond with sad feelings?	of how a person views
	Counter Example: Do you always	causation, sources, and
	feel sad when I do this?	origins—specifies
	How specifically does this work?	beliefs about how world works

12. Complex Equivalences
(Phenomena that differ which someone equates as the same)

"She's always yelling at me, she doesn't like me."	How do you equate her yelling as meaning she doesn't like you?	Recovers how the person equates or associates one
	Can you recall a time when you yelled at someone that you liked?	thing with another. Ask for counter-examples to
"He's a loser when it comes to business; he just lacks business sense."	How do you know to equate his lack of success in business with his lack of sense about it?	the meaning equation.
		Could other factors play a role in this?

13. Presuppositions
(Silent Assumptions, Unspoken Paradigms).

"If my husband knew how much I suffered, he would not do that."	How do you suffer? In what way? About what? How do you know that your husband doesn't know this? How is it that you assume that his intentions would shift if he knew? Does your husband always use your emotional state to determine his responses?	Recovers the person's assumptions, beliefs, and values the he or she just doesn't question. Specifies processes, nouns, verbs, etc. left out.

14. Over/Under Defined Terms (O/U)
"I married him because I thought he would make a good husband."	What behaviors and responses would make a "good" husband for you? do you use for the word "husband?"	Recover the extensional What references facts about the terms used.

15. Delusional Verbal Splits (DVS)
"My mind has nothing to do with this depression."	How can you have "mind" apart from "body" or "body" apart from "mind?"	Recovers the split that someone has created verbally in language

16. Either-or Phrases(E-O)
"If I don't make this relationship work, it proves my incompetence."	So you have no other alternative except total success or failure? You can't imagine any intermediate steps or stages?	Recovers the continuum deleted by the Either-Or structure

17. Multiordinality (M)
"What do you think of your self?"	On what level of abstraction do you refer to "self?"	Recovers the level of "Self" can have many different abstraction that the meanings, depending on context and usage—speaker operates from. how do you mean it? Specifies the context and order.

18. Static Words (SW)
"Science says that..." details	What science specifically? Science according to whose model or theory? Science at what time?	Recovers the deleted

19. Pseudo-words (PW)
"And that makes him a failure."	What do you mean by "failure" as a word that modifies a person?	Challenges a map that uses words that have no real referent.

20. Identification (Id.)

"He is a democrat." "She is a jerk."	How specifically does he identify with the term "democrat?" In what way? Upon what basis do you evaluate her using the term "jerk?"	Recovers the process of Identification or prediction. Invites one to create new generalizations.

21. Personalizing (Per.)

"He does that just to irritate me."	How do you know his intentions? How do you know to take these actions in a personal way?	Challenges the process of personalizing.

22. Metaphors (Mp)

"That reminds me of the time when Uncle John..."	How does this story relate to the point you want to make?	Recovers the isomorphic relationship between the story and the person's concepts.

Contacting The Author

L. Michael Hall currently lives in Colorado from where he writes and trains. He has authored numerous works in the field of NLP including:

The Spirit Of NLP: *The Process, Meaning And Criteria For Mastering NLP*

Meta States: *Self-Reflexiveness In Human States Of Consciousness*

Dragon Slaying: *Dragons To Princes*

Time-Lining: *Patterns For Adventuring In "Time"* (with Dr. Bob Bodenhamer)

Figuring Out People: *Design Engineering With Meta-Programs* (with Dr. Bodenhamer)

NLP: Going Meta—*Advance Modeling Using Meta-States*

How To Do What When—*A Wonderful Book Of Patterns* (with Barbara Belnap)

The Secrets Of Magic: *Communicational Excellence For The 21st Century*

Meta-States Journal (Write to Neuro-Semantic Institute for a free sample)

Centers in the UK and in the USA where you can catch training with Dr. Hall include:

> **Frank Daniels Associates**
> Frank Daniels
> 103 Hands Road, Heanor,
> Derbyshire DE75 7HB
> Tel/Fax: +44 1773 532 195

Post-Graduate Medical And Professional Education
Dr. Philip Nolan / Denis Bridoux,
St. Luke's Hospital
Blackmoorfoot Road
Huddersfield, West Yorkshire HD4 5RQ
+44 1484 654711 Ext. 3286 Fax: +44 1484 482409

Institute of Neuro-Semantics / ET Publications
L. Michael Hall, Ph. D.
1904 N. 7th. Street
Grand Junction, CO. 81501-7418
Tel. (970) 245-3235
/ NLPMetaStates@OnLineCol. com

NLP of Gastonia
Dr. Bobby G. Bodenhamer
1516 Cecilia Drive
Gastonia, NC. 28054
(704) 864-3585 Fax: (704) 864-1545
Http:/ /www. neurosemantics. com

The NLP Center of Texas
Rodas Haskell Associates, Inc.
Edit Rodas-Carroll
4600 Post Oak Place, Suite 204
Houston, TX. 77027
(713) 439-0011(800) 625-1925 Fax: (713) 439-0030

The Mind-Body Harmony Institute
Liz Redmond, NLP Trainer
6509 Government St. Suite C
Baton Rouge, LA. 70806
(504) 924-6533

The Anglo-American Book Company, Ltd.
Crown Buildings, Bancyfelin, Carmarthen, SA33 5ND
United Kingdom
(+44 (0) 1267 211880—Fax: +44 (0) 1267 211882
books@anglo-american. co. uk
http:/ /www. anglo-american. co. uk

Glossary Of Terms

Accessing Cues: The ways we tune our bodies by breathing, posture, gesture and eye movements to think in certain ways.

As-If Frame: Pretending that some event has happened, so thinking "as if" it had occurred, encourages creative problem-solving by mentally going beyond apparent obstacles to desired solutions.

Analogue: Continuously variable between limits, like a dimmer switch for a light. An analogue submodality varies like light to dark, while a digital submodality operates as either off or on, i. e. we see a picture in either an associated or dissociated way.

Anchoring: The process by which any stimulus or representation (external or internal) gets connected to and so triggers a response. Anchors occur naturally and intentionally (as in analogue marking). The NLP concept of anchoring derives from the Pavlovian stimulus-response reaction, classical conditioning. In Pavlov's study the tuning fork became the stimulus (anchor) that cued the dog to salivate.

Association: This refers to mentally seeing, hearing, and feeling from inside an experience. Associated contrasts with dissociated. In dissociation, you see a young you in the visual image. Generally, dissociation removes emotion from the experience while in association we experience the information emotionally.

Auditory: the sense of hearing, one of the basic Representation Systems.

Behavior: Any activity we engage in, micro like thinking, or macro like external actions.

Beliefs: thoughts, conscious or unconscious, which have grown into a generalization about causality, meaning, self, others, behaviors, identity, etc. Beliefs address the world and operating in it. Beliefs guide us in perceiving and interpreting reality. Beliefs relate closely to values. NLP has several belief change patterns.

Calibration: Becoming tuned-in to another's state via reading non-verbal signals previously observed and calibrated.

Chunking: Changing perception by going up or down levels and/or logical levels. Chunking up refers to going up a level (inducing up, induction). It leads to higher abstractions. Chunking down refers to going down a level (deducing, deduction). It leads to more specific examples or cases.

Complex Equivalence: A linguistic distinction wherein someone makes two statements to mean the same thing, e. g. "He is late; he doesn't love me."

Congruence: A state wherein one's internal representation works in an aligned way. What a person says corresponds with what s/he does. Both their non-verbal signals and their verbal statements match. A state of unity, fitness, internal harmony, not conflict.

Conscious: Present moment awareness. Awareness of seven +/- two chunks of information.

Content: The specifics and details of an event, answers *what?* and *why?* Contrasts with process or structure.

Context: The setting, frame or process in which events occur and provides meaning for content.

Cues: Information that provides clues to another's subjective structures, i. e. eye accessing cues, predicates, breathing, body posture, gestures, voice tone and tonality, etc.

Deletion:	The missing portion of an experience either linguistically or representationally.
Digital:	Varying between two states i. e. a light switch—either on or off. A digital submodality: color or black-and-white; an analogue submodality: varying between dark and bright.
Dissociation:	Not "in" an experience, but seeing or hearing it from outside as from a spectator's point of view, in contrast to association.
Distortion:	The modeling process by which we inaccurately represent something in our neurology or linguistics, can occur to create limitations or resources.
Downtime:	Not in sensory awareness, but "down" inside one's own mind seeing, hearing, and feeling thoughts, memories, awarenesses, a light trance state with attention focused inward.
Ecology:	The question about the overall relationship between idea, skill, response and larger environment or system. Internal ecology: the overall relationship between person and thoughts, strategies, behaviors, capabilities, values and beliefs. The dynamic balance of elements in a system.
Elicitation:	Evoking a state by word, behavior, gesture or any stimuli. Gathering information by direct observation of non-verbal signals or by asking meta-model questions.
Empowerment:	Process of adding vitality, energy, and new powerful resources to a person; vitality at the neurological level, change of habits.
Eye Accessing Cues:	Movements of the eyes in certain directions indicating visual, auditory or kinesthetic thinking (processing).
Epistemology:	The study of how we know what we know. NLP operates as an epistemology.

First Position:	Perceiving the world from your own point of view, associated, one of the three perceptual positions.
Frame:	Context, environment, meta-level, a way of perceiving something (as in Outcome Frame, "As If" Frame, Backtrack Frame, etc.).
Future Pace:	Process of mentally practicing (rehearsing) an event before it happens. One of the key processes for ensuring the permanency of an outcome, a frequent and key ingredient in most NLP interventions.
Generalization:	Process by which one specific experience comes to represent a whole class of experiences, one of the three modeling processes in NLP.
Gestalt:	A collection of memories connected neurologically based on similar emotions.
Hard Wired:	Neurologically based factor, the neural connectors primarily formed during gestation, similar to the hard wiring of a computer.
Incongruence:	State wherein parts conflict and war with each other, having reservations, not totally committed to an outcome, expressed in incongruent messages, signals, lack of alignment or matching of word and behavior.
Installation:	Process for putting a new mental strategy (way of doing things) inside mind-body so it operates automatically, often achieved through anchoring, leverage, metaphors, parables, reframing, future pacing, etc.
Internal Representations:	Patterns of information we create and store in our minds, combinations of sights, sounds, sensations, smells and tastes.
Kinesthetic:	Sensations, feelings, tactile sensations on surface of skin, proprioceptive sensations inside the body, includes vestibular system or sense of balance.

Leading:	Changing your own behaviors after obtaining rapport so another follows. An acid test for high level of rapport.
Logical Level:	A higher level, a level *about* a lower level, a meta-level that drives and modulates the lower level.
Loops:	A circle, cycle, a story, metaphor or representation that goes back to its own beginning, so that it loops back (feeds back) onto itself. An open loop: a story left unfinished. A closed loop: finishing a story. In strategies: loop refers to getting hung up in a set of procedures that have no way out, the strategy fails to exit.
Map of Reality:	Model of the world, a unique representation of the world built in each person's brain by abstracting from experiences, comprised of a neurological and a linguistic map, one's internal representations (IR).
Matching:	Adopting facets of another's outputs (behavior, words, etc.) to enhancing rapport.
Meta:	Above, beyond, about, at a higher level, a logical level higher.
Meta-model:	A model with 11 (or 12) linguistic distinctions that identify language patterns that obscure meaning in a communication via distortion, deletion and generalization. 11 (or 12) specific challenges or questions by which to clarify imprecise language (ill-formedness) to reconnect it to sensory experience and the deep structure. Meta-modeling brings a person out of trance. Developed, 1975, by Richard Bandler and John Grinder. Basis of all other discoveries in NLP.
Meta-Programs:	The mental/perceptual programs for sorting and paying attention to stimuli, perceptual filters that govern attention, sometimes "neuro-sorts," or meta-processes.

Meta-States: A state about a state, bringing a state of mind-body (fear, anger, joy, learning) to bear upon another state from a higher logical level, generates a gestalt state—a meta-state, developed by Michael Hall.

Mismatching: Offering different patterns of behavior to another, breaking rapport for the purpose of redirecting, interrupting, or terminating a meeting or conversation, mismatching as a meta-programs.

Modal Operators: Linguistic distinctions in the Meta-model that indicate the "mode" by which a person "operates"—the mode of necessity, impossibility, desire, possibility, etc., the predicates (can, can't, possible, impossible, have to, must, etc.) that we utilize for motivation.

Model: A description of how something works, a generalized, deleted or distorted copy of the original.

Modeling: A process of observing and replicating the successful actions and behaviors of others, the process of discerning the sequence of IR and behaviors that enable someone to accomplish a task, the basis of accelerated learning.

Model of the World: A map of reality, a unique representation of the world via abstraction from our experiences, the total of one's personal operating principles.

Multiple Description: The process of describing the same thing from different viewpoints.

Neuro-Linguistic Programming: The study of excellence, a model of how people structure their experience, the structure of subjective experience, how humans become *programmed* in their thinking-emoting and behaving in their very *neurology* by the various *languages* they use to process, code and retrieve information.

Nominalization: A linguistic distinction in the Meta-model, a hypnotic pattern of trance language, a process or verb turned into an (abstract) noun, a process frozen in time.

Outcome:	A specific, sensory-based desired result. Should meet the well-formedness criteria.
Pacing:	Gaining and maintaining rapport with another by joining their model of the world by saying what fits with and matches their language, beliefs, values, current experience, etc. Crucial to rapport building.
Parts:	Unconscious parts, sub-personalities created through some Significant Emotional Experience (SEE), disowned and separated functions that begin to take on a life of their own, a source of intra-personal conflict when incongruent.
Perceptual Filters:	Unique ideas, experiences, beliefs, values, meta-programs, decisions, memories and language that shape and color our model of the world.
Perceptual Position:	One's point of view of five positions. First Position: associated from one's own eyes. Second Position: from the listener's perspective. Third Position: from a meta-position outside self and other, neutral observer. Fourth Position: we, seeing from the viewpoint of the group, system, or organization. Fifth Position: simultaneous and systemically incorporating all four perceptual positions, the God viewpoint.
Physiological:	The physical part of the person.
Predicates:	What we assert or predicate about a subject, sensory based words indicating a particular RS (visual predicates, auditory, kinesthetic, unspecified).
Preferred System:	The RS that an individual typically uses most in thinking and organizing experience.
Presuppositions:	Ideas that we have to take for granted for a communication to make sense, assumptions, that which "holds" (position) "up" (sup) a statement "ahead of time" (pre).

Rapport:	A sense of connection with another, a feeling of mutuality, a sense of trust, created by pacing, mirroring and matching, a state of empathy or second position.
Reframing:	Taking a frame-of-reference so that it looks new or different, presenting an event or idea from a different point of view so it has a different meaning; content or context reframing, a change pattern.
Representation:	An idea, thought, presentation of sensory-based or evaluative based information.
Representation System (RS):	How we mentally code information using the sensory systems: Visual, Auditory, Kinesthetic, Olfactory, and Gustatory.
Requisite Variety:	Flexibility in thinking, emoting, speaking, behaving; the person with the most flexibility of behavior controls the action; the Law of Requisite Variety.
Resources:	Any means we can bring to bear to achieve an outcome: physiology, states, thoughts, strategies, experiences, people, events or possessions.
Resourceful State:	The total neurological and physical experience when a person feels resourceful.
Satir Categories:	The five body postures and language styles indicating specific ways of communicating: leveler, blamer, placater, computer and distracter, developed by Virginia Satir, Family Therapist.
Second Position:	Perceiving the world from another's point of view, in tune with another's sense of reality.
Sensory Acuity:	Awareness of the outside world, of the senses, making finer distinctions about the sensory information we get from the world.
Sensory-Based Description:	Information directly observable and verifiable by the senses, see-hear-feel language that we can test empirically, in contrast to evaluative descriptions.

"Sleight of Mouth"   Numerous reframing patterns that allow a
Patterns: person to transform meaning conversationally.
Similar to "sleight of hand" patterns, we make
a "frame-of-reference" move that the listener
doesn't notice.

State: Holistic phenomenon of mind-body-emotions,
mood, emotional condition; sum total of all
neurological and physical processes within
individual at any moment in time.

Strategy: A sequencing of thinking-behaving to obtain
an outcome or create an experience, the struc-
ture of subjectivity ordered in a linear model of
the TOTE.

Submodality: Distinctions within each RS, qualities of
internal representations, the smallest building
blocks of thoughts, characteristics in each
system.

Synesthesia: Automatic link from one RS to another, a V-K
synesthesia involves seeingfeeling without a
moment of consciousness to think about it,
automatic program.

Third Position: Perceiving world from viewpoint of an
observer's position, one of the three perceptual
positions; position where you see both yourself
and another.

Time-line: A metaphor describing how we store our
sights, sounds and sensations of memories and
imaginations, a way of coding and processing
the construct "time."

T. O. T. E.   A flow-chart model developed by George
Miller and associates (Galanter & Pribram) to
explain the sequential processes that generate a
response. **Test-Operate-Test-Exit** updated the
Stimulus—Response model of behaviorism
which NLP further updated by adding RS.

Unconscious:	Everything not in conscious awareness, minor RS.
Universal Quantifiers:	A linguistic term in the Meta-model for words that code things with "allness" (every, all, never, none, etc.), a distinction that admits no exceptions.
Unsanity:	Used by Korzybski to describe the stage of poor adjustment between sanity (well adjusted to the territory) and insanity (totally maladjusted to reality). He defined it as "lack of consciousness of abstracting, confusion of orders of abstractions resulting from identification ... practically universally operating in every one of us" (1933: 105).
Unspecified Nouns:	Nouns that do not specify to whom or to what they refer.
Unspecified Verbs:	Verbs that have the adverb deleted, delete specifics of the action.
Uptime:	State where attention and senses directed outward to immediate environment, all sensory channels open and alert.
VAK:	A short-hand for the sensory representation systems of **V**isual, **A**uditory, and **K**inesthetic. The last one (K) including smells (Olfactory) and tastes (Gustatory).
Value:	What we deem as important in a particular context. Our values or criteria motivate us and arise from our valuing.
Visual:	Seeing, imagining; the RS of sight.
Visualization:	The process of seeing images in your mind.
Well-Formedness Condition:	The criteria that enable us to specify an outcome in ways that make it achievable and verifiable; powerful tool for negotiating win/win solutions.

Bibliography

Bacon, Francis. (1620) *Instauratio Magna. Novum Organum.* London: John Bill Publishing.

Bandler, Richard; and Grinder, John. (1975) *The Structure Of Magic, Volume I: A Book About Language And Therapy.* Palo Alto, CA: Science and Behavior Books.

Bandler, Richard and Grinder, John. (1979) *Frogs Into Princes: Neuro-Linguistic Programming.* Moab, UT: Real People Press.

Bandler, Richard and Grinder, John. (1982) *Reframing: Neuro-Linguistic Programming And The Transformation Of Meaning.* Moab, UT: Real People Press.

Bandler, Richard. (1985) *Magic In Action.* Capitola, CA: Meta Publications Inc.

Bandler, Richard. (1985) *Using Your Brain For A Change: Neuro-Linguistic Programming.* Moab, UT: Real People Press.

Bandler, Richard. (1987) *Paranoid Schizophrenia, Parts I & II.* Video-tape. Arvada, CO: NLP Comprehensive.

Bartlett, F. C. (1932) *Remembering: An Experimental And Social Study.* Cambridge, England: Cambridge University Press.

Bateson, Gregory. (1979) *Mind And Nature: A Necessary Unity.* New York: Ballantine.

Bateson, Gregory. (1972) *Steps To An Ecology Of Mind.* New York: Ballantine.

Beck, A. T. (1976) *Cognitive Therapy And The Emotional Disorders.* New York: International University Press.

Bodenhamer, Bobby G.; and L. Michael Hall (1997) *Time-lining: Advanced Patterns In "Time" Processes.* Wales, UK: Anglo-American Book Co. Ltd.

Bourland, David D. Jr., Johnston, Paul Dennithorne; and Klein, Jeremy. (1994) *More E-prime: To Be Or Not II.* Concord, CA: International Society for General Semantics.

Carroll, John B. (Ed.) (1956) *Language, Thought, And Reality: Selected Writings Of Benjamin Lee Whorf.* New York: Wiley.

Chomsky, Noam. (1957) *Syntactic Structures.* The Hague: Mouton Publishers.

Chomsky, Noam. (1965) *Aspects Of The Theory Of Syntax.* Cambridge, MA: MIT Press.

de Shazer, Steve. (1988) *Clues: Investigating Solutions In Brief Therapy.* New York: Norton.

de Shazer, Steve. (1991) *Putting Difference To Work.* New York: Norton.

de Shazer, Steve. (1994) *Words Were Originally Magic.* New York: Norton.

Dilts, Robert; Grinder, John; Bandler, Richard; DeLozier, Judith. (1980) *Neuro-Linguistic Programming, Volume I: The Study Of The Structure Of Subjective Experience.* Capitola. CA: Meta Publications Inc.

Dilts, Robert. (1983a) *Applications Of Neuro-Linguistic Programming.* Capitola. CA: Meta Publications Inc.

Dilts, Robert B. (1983b) *Roots Of Neuro-Linguistic Programming.* Capitola. CA: Meta Publications Inc.

Ellis, Albert. (1962) *Reason And Emotion In Psychotherapy.* New York: Lyle Stuart.

Ellis, Albert. (1973) **Humanistic Psychotherapy:** *The Rational-Emotive Approach.* New York: Julian Press.

Ellis, Albert and Harper, Robert A. (1976) *A New Guide To Rational Living.* Englewood Cliffs, NJ: Prentice-Hall, Inc.

Efran, J. S. Lukens, M. D., and Lukens, R. J. (1990) **Language Structure And Change.** New York: Norton.

Frankl, V. E. (1957/1984) **Man's Search For Meaning:** *An Introduction To Logotherapy.* (3rd. ed.) New York: Simon & Schuster.

Freud, Sigmund. (1915-1917) **The Complete Introductory Lectures On Psychoanalysis** (J. Stachey, Ed. & Trans.) **The Standard Edition Of The Complete Psychological Works Of Sigmund Freud** (Vol. 15 & 16) New York: Norton.

Gilliland, Burl E., James, Richard K., and Bowman, James T. (1989) **Theories And Strategies In Counseling And Psychology.** (2nd. ed.) NJ: Prentice Hall.

Grinder, John; and Judith DeLozier. (1987) **Turtles All The Way Down:** *Prerequisites To Personal Genius.* Scotts Valley, CA: Grinder & Associates.

Grinder, John; and Bandler, Richard. (1976) **The Structure Of Magic, II.** Palo Alto, CA: Science & Behavior Books.

Gross, Maurice. (1979) On The Failure Of Generative Grammar. **Language, Vol. 55**, No. 4, pp. 859-885. Baltimore: Linguistic Society of America.

Hall, Michael L. (1995) **Meta-states:** *A New Domain Of Logical Levels, Self-Reflexiveness In Human States Of Consciousness.* Grand Junction, CO: ET Publications.

Hall, L. Michael (1996a) **The Spirit Of NLP:** *The Process, Meaning, And Criteria For Mastering NLP.* Wales, UK: Anglo-American Book Co. Ltd.

Hall, L. Michael (1996b) *Dragon Slaying: Dragons To Princes.* Grand Jct. CO: ET Publications.

Hall, Michael L. (1996c) *Becoming A Ferocious Presenter.* Grand Jct. CO: ET Publications.

Hall, Michael L. (1996d) *Languaging: The Linguistics Of Psychotherapy.* Grand Jct. CO: ET Publ.

Hall, Michael L. (1997) *Figuring Out People: Design Engineering With Meta-Programs.* Wales, UK: Anglo-American Book Co. Ltd.

Hall, L. Michael. (1997a) *Neuro-Linguistic Programming: Going Meta—Advance Modeling Using Meta-States & Logical Levels.* Grand Jct. CO: ET Publ.

Hayakawa, S. I. (1941/ 1980) *Language In Action.* New York: Harcourt, Brace, & Co.

Harris, Randy Allen. (1993) *The Linguistic Wars.* NY: Oxford University Press.

Huxley, Aldous (1954) *The Doors Of Perception And Heaven And Hell.* NY: Harper & Row.

Jackendoff, Ray. (1994) *Patterns In The Mind: Language and human nature.* New York: Basic Books, Harper-Collins Publishers.

Jacobson, Sid. (1989) *Meta-Cation. Volume II: New Improved Formulas For Thinking About Thinking.* Capitola, CA: Meta Publications Inc.

Johnson, Wendell (1964/1989) *People In Quandaries: The Semantics Of Personal Adjustment.* San Franciso, CA: International Society For General Semantics.

Kelly, George A. (1955) *The Psychology Of Personal Constructs.* New York: Norton.

Korzybski, Alfred. (1933/ 1994) *Science And Sanity: An Introduction To Non-Aristotelian Systems And General Semantics,* (5th. ed.) Lakeville, CN: International Non-Aristotelian Library Publishing Co.

Korzybski, Alfred (1949) Fate And Freedom. In Lee, Irving, J. (Ed.) *The Language Of Wisdom And Folly.* New York: Harper & Brothers.

Korzybski, A. (1990) *Collected Writings: 0291-0591.* Kendig, M. and Read, C. S. (Eds.) Englewood, NJ: Institute of General Semantics.

Lakoff, George; and Johnson, Mark. (1980) *Metaphors We Live By.* Chicago: The University of Chicago Press.

Lakoff, George. (1987) *Women, Fire, And Dangerous Things: What Categories Reveal About The Mind.* Chicago: The University of Chicago Press.

Langacker, Ronald W. (1987) *Foundations Of Cognitive Grammar, Vol. 1.* Stanford, CA: Stanford University Press.

Langacker, Ronald W. (1991) *Concept, Image And Symbol: The Cognitive Basis Of Grammar.* New York: Mouton de Gruyter.

Lankton, Stephen R. (1980) *Practical Magic: A Translation Of Basic NLP Into Clinical Psychotherapy.* Capitola, CA: Meta Publications Inc.

Lewis, A. Bryon; and Pucelik, R. Frank. (1982) *Magic Demystified: A Pragmatic Guide To Communication And Change.* Portland, OR: Metamorphous Advanced Product Services.

Lisnek, Paul M. (1996) *Winning The Mind Game: Negotiating In Business And Life.* Capitola, CA: Meta Publications Inc.

Mandler, George; and Kessen, William. (1975) *The Language Of Psychology.* NY: Robert E. Krieger Publishing Co.

McClendon, Terrence L. (1989) *The Wild Days: NLP 1972 to 1981.* Capitola, CA: Meta Publications.

McLauchlin, Larry. (1993) *Advanced Language Patterns Mastery.* Calgary, Alberta, Canada: Leading Edge Communications.

McMaster, Michael; Grinder, John. (1983/1993) *Precision: A New Approach To Communication—How To Get The Information You Need To Get Results.* Scotts Valley, CA: Grinder, Delozier & Associates.

Miller, George. (1956) *The Magical Number Seven, Plus Or Minus Two: Some Limits On Our Capacity To Process Information. Psychological Review, 63,* 81-97.

O'Connor, Joseph; and Seymour, John. (1990) *Introducing Neuro-Linguistic Programming: The New Psychology Of Personal Excellence.* London, UK: Thorsons.

Perls, Fritz. (1973) *The Gestalt Approach And Eye Witness To Therapy.* Palo Alto, CA: Science and Behavior Books, Inc.

Pfalzgraf, Rene. (1989)"*Meta-Model III.*"Rapporter. May, 1989. Cottonwood, AZ.

Piaget, J. and Inhelder, B. (1956) *The Child's Conception Of Space.* London: UK: Routledge & Kegan Paul.

Robins, Anthony (1989) *Unlimited Power: The New Science Of Personal Achievement.* NY: Simon and Schuster.

Robbins, Anthony (1991) *Awaken The Giant Within: How To Take Immediate Control Of Your Mental, Emotional, Physical, & Financial Destiny!* NY: Simon & Schuster.

Satir, Virginia. (1972) *Peoplemaking.* Palo Alto, CA: Science and Behavior Books, Inc.

Spitzer, Robert S. (1992) Virginia Satir and Origins of NLP. *Anchor Point Magazine* (July, 1992), pp. 40-44. Franktown, CO: Cahill Mountain Press.

Vaihinger, H. (1924) *The Philosophy Of 'As If. '* *A System Of The Theoretical, Practical, And Religious Fictions Of Mankind.* (Translated by C. K. Ogden) New York: Harcourt, Brace.

Wilber, Ken. (1983) *Eye To Eye: The Quest For The New Paradigm.* Garden City, New York: Anchor Press/Doubleday.

Yeager, Joseph. (1985) *Thinking About Thinking With NLP.* Capitola, CA: Meta Publications Inc.

Zink, Nelson; and Munshaw, Joseph. (1995) Collapsing Generalizations and the Other Half of NLP. *NLP World* (Vol. 3. No. 1) Switzerland.

L. Michael Hall, PhD earned his doctorate in Cognitive-Behavioral Psychology with a special emphasis in linguistics and wrote his dissertation, Languaging: The Linguistics of Psychotherapy, has a masters in Clinical Psychology, another masters in biblical language and literature, and a bachelor of science in Management of Human Resources. From his studies with Richard Bandler in the late 1980s, he wrote *The Spirit of NLP* on mastering the process, meaning, and criteria of NLP. Among his other contributions to NLP, he has developed the Meta-States Model, and then with Dr. Bob Bodenhamer applied the principle of systemic logical levels to meta-programs, time-lines, and "sleight of mouth" patterns. Currently Michael lives in Colorado as a single father with a teenage daughter, Jessica, where they hike, rollerblade, and enjoy the mountains.

Crown House Publishing

(A division of The Anglo-American Book Company Ltd.)
Crown Buildings,
Bancyfelin,
Carmarthen SA33 5ND
Wales.
Telephone: 01267 211880 / 211886
Fax: 01267 211882

We trust you enjoyed this title from our range of bestselling books for academic and general readership. Our authors are professionals of many years' experience, all highly respected in their own field. We choose our books with care for their content and character, and for the value of their contribution of both new and updated material to their particular field. Here is a list of our other publications.

Figuring Out People: *Design Engineering With Meta-Programs*
  by Bob G. Bodenhamer & L. Michael Hall   Paperback   £12.99

Gold Counselling: *A Practical Psychology With NLP*
  by Georges Philips   Paperback   £14.99

Grieve No More, Beloved: *The Book Of Delight*
  by Ormond McGill   Hardback   £9.99

Influencing With Integrity: *Management Skills For Communication & Negotiation*
  by Genie Z Laborde   Paperback   £12.50

Living Organisations: *Beyond The Learning Organisation*
  by Lex McKee   Hardback   £16.99

The New Encyclopedia Of Stage Hypnotism
  by Ormond McGill   Hardback   £29.99

The POWER Process: *An NLP Approach To Writing*
  by Sid Jacobson & Dixie Elise Hickman   Paperback   £12.99

Scripts & Strategies In Hypnotherapy
  by Roger P. Allen   Hardback   £19.99

Slimming With Pete: *Taking The Weight Off Body AND Mind*
  by Pete Cohen & Judith Verity   Paperback   £9.99

Seeing The Unseen: *A Past Life Revealed Through Hypnotic Regression*
  by Ormond McGill   Paperback   £12.99

Solution States: *A Course In Solving Problems In Business Using NLP*
  by Sid Jacobson   Paperback   £12.99

The Spirit Of NLP: *The Process, Meaning And Criteria For Mastering NLP*
  by L. Michael Hall   Paperback   £12.99

Time-Lining: *Patterns For Adventuring In "Time"*
  by Bob G. Bodenhamer & L. Michael Hall   Paperback   £14.99

Vibrations For Health And Happiness: *Everyone's Easy Guide To Stress-free Living*
  by A M Tom Bolton   Paperback   £9.99